THE RADICAL CHURCH

Restoring the Apostolic Edge

Bryn Jones

Destiny Image® Publishers, Inc.
P.O. Box 310
Shippensburg, PA 17257-0310

"Speaking to the Purposes of God for This Generation
and for the Generations to Come"

ISBN 0-7684-2022-9

For Worldwide Distribution
Printed in the U.S.A.

This book and all other Destiny Image, Revival Press,
and Treasure House books are available
at Christian bookstores and distributors worldwide.

For a U.S. bookstore nearest you, call **1-800-722-6774**.
For more information on foreign distributors, call **717-532-3040**.
Or reach us on the Internet: **http://www.reapernet.com**

Acknowledgments

I WISH TO EXPRESS my sincere thanks to my wife Edna and to my family for standing with me in the costly journey of this vision. Thanks also to Caroline Okell for her many hours of typing and re-typing. I also thank John Maggos for reading and critiquing the manuscript, and thanks to the many colleagues whom I work with daily and through whom much that I have written has been proven. Finally, thanks to all my friends and enemies who have spurred me forward in the pursuit of the kind of Church I write about here.

Endorsements

"Against the backdrop of a deteriorating society, Bryn Jones paints a picture of hope. As a new millennium approaches, the Church is seen as the sharp end of an advancing Kingdom where the covenant promises of God still hold true.

"We are lifted to see the 'cosmic' purposes of God unfold through the restoration and release of ministries and gifts into every sphere of our fallen world."

—Stuart Bell
New Life Christian Fellowship
Newland-Lincoln, England

"If you think you know Bryn Jones, this book will surprise you. He approaches reconstructionism and the 'Jewish issue' with significant wisdom and insight. If you don't know him, you will wish you had read more of his writings before now. If you are looking for apostolic Christianity, this book will help you enormously."

—Gerald Coates
Pioneer, Speaker, Author, Broadcaster
United Kingdom

"In *The Radical Church* we have the insights of a leading statesman, guiding us through a restoration perspective of God's involvement in the world through the Church."

—Rev. Joel Edwards, General Director
Evangelical Alliance
United Kingdom

"This book is destined to become a handbook for every church leader who longs for his church to impact our society as the early Church in Acts did. Bryn Jones' deep understanding of the Scriptures shines through the pages of *The Radical Church*, giving the reader a desire to see the Church of God emerge as the living Body of Christ and challenging him on some traditional views he may have on 'the Church.' Thank you, Bryn, for being obedient to God in releasing this timely book!"

—Ken Gott
Revival Now!
Sunderland, United Kingdom

"Bryn Jones compares the current condition of the Church to the original intention of God's Church. Bryn shows what the Church is supposed to be in stark contrast to what it is. As he says, 'Ours is not the backward look of nostalgia, hoping to find a dubious mythological perfection in the early Church.' Today we seek to find those elements that are the foundational part of the process of advancing the Church into its fullness and maturity.

"He calls for a heavenly harmony where earth begins to sing on pitch with heaven's tune...where man prays the Lord's prayers instead of man's prayers. Layer by layer Bryn peals away the onion skin of the modern problems of the Church. He shows that this modern problem parallels the problems of the primitive Church. Man is the same, but God is also the same, and the Church must not abandon her hope for tomorrow. In Bryn's words, 'Is it not time for passionate prophetic confrontation again?' "

—Tommy Tenney
Revivalist and Author of *The God Chasers*
Louisiana

Contents

Foreword

Having known Bryn Jones for more than 20 years, I was honored when asked to write the foreword for his book. I have watched Bryn travel throughout the world declaring the message contained in this book. It has transformed lives. It has given God's people hope for the future. It has lifted us up into the higher realm of God's purposes throughout history.

Over a decade ago I was asked who I most identified with in ministry today. Unhesitatingly I responded that it was Bryn Jones. This man has been a hero in the faith to me and multitudes of others worldwide. For those who have never had the privilege of meeting this man in person, I trust that this book will serve you well.

Launching into the third millennium, God has graciously supplied His people with a clear and concise blueprint for His purpose. *The Radical Church* is must reading for everyone committed to "keeping in step with the Spirit" (Gal. 5:25) in these historic days. Thanks, Bryn, for both the book and your life that backs it up!

Larry Tomczak
Christian leader, church planter, author,
and teacher at the Brownsville School of Revival

Preface

Why This Book?

AS WE CROSS THE FRONTIERS into the third millennium, we find ourselves in a very different world than that of the peoples of the first millennium. The simple world of the farmer, fisherman, carpenter, and tentmaker has given way to the world of the Internet, IT satellites, space probes, and genetically engineered and altered animals and food products. Computerization in every field continues to increase human knowledge at an incredible speed, which in turn continues to force society into ever quicker and more radical adjustments. Unfortunately, the legitimate desire for scientific progress is threatening to push the boundaries of our exploration beyond what is morally acceptable. The specter of a fully planned society with controlled birth and death now looms on the horizon, and the stress levels associated with our quickly changing times leaves humanity critically threatened with overload.

The challenge to the Church as we approach the third millennium is to demonstrate the life and power of God in this new generation, showing the relevance of the gospel to the highly complex needs of our fast-developing scientific and intellectual generation. In a generation demanding reality and relevance, we Christians must ask ourselves, Is the image of Christ we project a true one? Is our understanding of the Church accurate? Are we trapped by its image of the Christ of the icon? Does a vision of the crucifix still dominate our minds? Is our view of the Church still the building on the corner or the ornate cathedral in the center of the city? When we speak of ministry, do we think of professional clergy, vicar, or priest in his vestments, or even an articulate, high profile entrepreneurial TV pastor or evangelist?

Communicating the life of God effectively to our world requires that we look at ourselves and ask ourselves these specific questions: Are we the Church Jesus gave Himself for, or are we some poor twentieth century replica of it? Are we doing things His way or our own? Sadly, the suggestion that we ask these questions is often met with such sharp retorts as: "Let's not argue about Church government or methods; we are all seeking the same goal—the gospel to the whole earth. Let's concentrate on that rather than on any 'form' or 'structure' that is of minor importance. It's the power of God that matters."

On the surface, this statement might appear reasonable, perhaps even magnanimously all-inclusive, but is it biblically accurate? Is God unconcerned with how His Church is built?

When God told Moses to build a tabernacle, He printed its blueprint deep into His servant's mind and soul; Moses was told to build it "according to the pattern shown" (Ex. 25:40). God's requirements concerning materials, measurements, and ministry reveal a divine concern for detail. Every "pin" and "socket" was according to pattern. The fact is, *nothing* about the tabernacle's construction—or the ministry associated with it—was left to personal opinion or judgment; it was not to be done just any old way.

Consider the temple that Solomon built according to the plans revealed to his father David—plans that were written by "the hand of the Lord" (1 Chron. 28:19). The intricacy involved in constructing the temple required the employment of very skilled craftsmen to get it right. The order of priesthood, the sacrifices, and even the singing associated with the temple were all done according to God's direction. Can we really believe that God would show such concern for a tabernacle and temple—"shadows" of the greater reality (see Heb. 8:5)—and then suspend all requirements concerning His Church, its ministry, and its ordering today?

These biblical records do not sound like form and structure are unimportant to God; in fact, even a cursory survey of the New Testament reveals that we simply cannot afford to think that God will tolerate slapstick efforts to build on top of His costly foundation. The apostle Paul took great care in laying a true foundation of understanding and practice of the life of Christ in the early Church, and he warns those who would follow to "be careful how they build upon it" (see 1 Cor. 3:10 NAS).

Thankfully, we can confidently say that God is infusing His people in this generation with a renewed sense of the divine mind and capturing their hearts with His purpose. As Moses' heart burned with a desire to build what he saw on the mountain, so many of God's people today are aflame with a passion to build according to His plan in their generation. They are the repairers and *restorers* for our time.

*Your ancient ruins shall be rebuilt; you shall raise up the foundations of many generations; you shall be called **the repairer of the breach, the restorer of streets to live in*** (Isaiah 58:12 NRS).

Such people believe that God will bring His plan to completion in a single generation and release the greatest spiritual awakening ever known.

That's what this book is all about.

Chapter 1

Free From Religion's Web

*All it takes to make sure nothing changes
is to settle for things as they are.*

THE CHURCH has never been as numerically strong or as globally widespread as it is today. Christianity is presently the world's largest religion—with 1.6 billion adherents. Yet, as we prepare to enter the third millennium, the Church is wrestling within itself to identify both its moral base in a culture that has generally abandoned moral absolutes and its role in a world that tends to view the religious establishment as irrelevantly archaic. Internally riddled with dissension, the Church's testimony

1

has become blunted by mediocrity and its voice muted by compromise. As a result, today's Church is in danger of simply meandering across the millennial line, having lost sight of God's original purpose.

The crisis of the Church is serious, and it must be successfully confronted if the Church is to be in the next millennium what it was in the first: a light shining in the darkness of the moral maze and the hand of God reaching out to heal the sick, bless the underclass, lift the downtrodden, and give hope and life to the hurting masses.

A Historical Overview

To be sure, this is not the first time that the Church has faced millennial or generational crisis. From its very beginning, from both within and without, the Church has had to grapple with ideas and beliefs contrary to the purpose of God's will. The incarnation itself presented a crisis moment for the Jewish nation. All those in the faith of Abraham were faced with decision, and despite the fact that the majority in Judaism rejected Christ, those in the true line of faith in Israel responded to Him as their Messiah.

Crisis again erupted in the early Church over the issue of circumcision. Teachers from Jerusalem traveled throughout Galatia, contending that it was necessary for the Gentile believers to be circumcised to be truly accepted as people of God. This provoked the formation of the first church council, which was assembled to bring resolve to the matter in a way that preserved the unity of the churches—at least for a time.

Successive crises from that time until now have resulted in further upheavals, divisions, church councils, and even reformation. Through it all, there have always been people committed to the quest for unity, believing that there would be a "restoration of all things spoken of by the prophets" before Christ would return (see Acts 3:21 NAS), and spiritual movements throughout history have re-quickened this hope. The Moravians, Anabaptists, early Franciscans of Assisi, Christian Disciples, and—at the close of the last century—the Christian Brethren, were all rooted in a *restorationist* philosophy. Often rejected and persecuted, they nevertheless kept hope alive throughout succeeding generations, and they remained determined that Christianity would not be buried in the shrouds of institutional religion. They strove to fulfill the purpose of God in manifesting the fullness of Christ in the life and works of His Church. Evangelicals, Pentecostals, Charismatics, and to some extent the discipleship, faith, deliverance, prophetic, and renewal movements of our time, have all helped to fuel a new spirit of inquiry, a new intercessory passion, a heightened expectation and faith for the "restoration of all things" to happen in this generation.

Where Are We Today?

The crisis currently facing the Church—although similar in some respects to those that have preceded it—is also different to any previously encountered in history. The 1960's, dominated by the quest for a meaningful spiritual experience, gave rise to various kinds of religious groups. These groups ranged from those representing the fringes of Christianity to those oriented toward Eastern mystic religions. The Jesus People, The Way, Children of God, Hari Krishna, Divine Light, Scientology, and the rise of New Ageism all competed for the minds and souls of people. In addition to the spiritual searching reflected in the popularity of these cults and groups, today's generation has now come to accept the paranormal, the psychic, the occult, and the many differing aspects of spiritualistic activity in an unprecedented way. This truth confronts us with a deepening crisis that we cannot afford to dismiss or ignore.

If people are to see the Church as something other than a "dinosaurian relic" in the world of the third millennium, then we, the Church, must be willing to discard all irrelevant religious baggage and strip ourselves of all biblically insupportable practices in the process. We must become passionately clear and decisive on the moral issues of our time. If we are to be relevant to the need and search of mankind, then we must rediscover our true mission in order to capture this present post-industrial generation. We must rediscover and reaffirm our commitment to the integrity of the gospel and the manifestation of the dynamic power of God in ministry.

As God's people, we believe that He intends something significant to happen in this generation that will restore the message and ministry of Jesus and the Christian communities of 2,000 years ago and that will take us forward to realities and maturity that the early Church never saw. This demands a willingness to change on our part. Successive revivals have highlighted the Spirit's call for change, not for the sake of change, but to recover lost ground, to realign ourselves with divine purpose, and to continue the process of the restoration of all things. *It is not enough for us to try harder and harder to do old things better and better; **we must change**.* It is also not sufficient to initiate change just on the periphery of our meetings, methodology, music leadership style, etc. Rather, it must occur at the very core of our thinking and practice. Such changes are painful, disruptive, and costly, which is why many people initially resist or resent such shifts in thought and action.

In the struggle for freedom and equality, Dr. Martin Luther King, Jr., in his *Letter From the Birmingham*

Jail, written on April 16, 1963, highlighted the pain of change in a most gripping and heart-wrenching way:

> "We know through painful experience that free-dom is never voluntarily given by the oppressor; it must be demanded by the oppressed. Frankly I have never yet engaged in a direct-action movement that was 'well-timed,' according to the timetable of those who have not suffered undu-ly from the disease of segregation. For years now I have heard the word 'Wait!' It rings in the ear of every Negro with a piercing familiarity. This 'wait' has almost always meant 'never.' It has been a tranquilizing thalidomide, relieving the emotional stress for a moment, only to give birth to an ill-formed infant of frustration. We must come to see with the distinguished jurist of yes-terday that 'justice too long delayed is justice denied.' "[1]

To enter the third millennium we must be sharp, anointed, and ready in every respect for its chal-lenges, and we must *actively* seek to return to those biblical principles that will enable us to be all that God intends us to be.

---

1. Martin Luther King, Jr., *Letter From the Birmingham Jail,* in F.W. Hale, Jr., ed., *The Cry for Freedom* (London: T. Yoseloff Ltd., 1969), 359.

Christianity is not a system of beliefs; it is men and women filled with the life of God—living their lives *His* way, doing *His* will endued with *His* Spirit, demonstrating *His* power, and performing *His* works amongst men. For God's covenant communities to fully emerge in this way will require a spiritual, moral, and intellectual revolution. As *restorers* we do not find this a daunting prospect. On the contrary, it is the very thing for which we live in active faith. We are entering the third millennium as the extension of the living Christ. The religious world is mistaken if it thinks that it can push what is being said by today's apostles and prophets into a corner and simply label it as "restorationist" doctrines or churches. *God is not after restorationist churches: He is restoring His Church.*

Chapter 2

Prisoners of Divine Purpose

Whom heaven must receive until the period of restoration of all things about which God spoke by the mouth of His holy prophets from ancient time (Acts 3:21 NAS).

AT THE CONCLUSION of the convention, people gathered in small, animated groups that were immersed in conversation. The general consensus was that the speaker had done an outstanding job of highlighting the main issues relevant to the times in the light of the impending return of Jesus Christ. As I was discussing what we had heard with a young Baptist pastor, he grew increasingly agitated by my responses to his very pessimistic dispensationalist view of the endtimes. Finally, he looked at me in frustration and sharply said, "Your problem is that you have a one-string fiddle. Every time we get into a serious conversation, you bring everything round to 'restoration' being the answer to the whole thing. I don't understand how you can be so naïve."

You may have heard others say similar things. But let's face it, without apology, the message Jesus brought to our world is simple; it is straightforward and plain to the everyday man and woman in the street. The fact that it is simple, however, does not weaken its demands or make it less profound. Neither does its simplicity detract from its radical nature or diminish its power.

Jesus chose His disciples from a broad spectrum of life and revealed God and His Kingdom to them in a way that made them prisoners of the divine purpose. He cut through the web of legalistic religious traditions that had obscured the simplicity of truth. The ordinary people loved His message of the Kingdom. They heard Him gladly and flocked *en masse* to where they could be with Him. They were warmly embraced by His compassionate heart, lifted from their misery, healed of their sicknesses, set free from demonic powers, and introduced to a new way of life.

Prisoners of Divine Purpose

Moving from the Gospel records of Jesus' ministry to the historical accounts of the Church in Acts, the story is one of continuing liberty and power in the life of the early Church. Emerging within the larger community of the world was a new kind of community. It was not based on racial, ethnic, or cultural similarities, but upon the love of God. It is not surprising that this Christian community found the same favor with the mass of disenfranchised, distressed, and dispersed peoples that Jesus did. Its residents proclaimed a new life, a new power, a new rule of God in the earth. Before long it was being said that these early Christians had "turned the world upside down" (Acts 17:6 KJV).

Sadly, the simplicity of early Christianity has long since disappeared. Today we are faced with highly organized and complex religious denominations—some 250,000 of them—and possibly as many independent groups. Their traditions are often more permanent than their testimony; their legalism stifles their liberty; their competitive attitudes negate their compassion; their wealth obscures their worship; and position is more sought after than purpose. Where is the Church of the Acts of the Apostles? Was it inevitable that the passage of time would defeat God's purpose in His people? Have cultural forces, bureaucracy, and technological realities become stronger than the Spirit in God's Church? Has the Church abandoned its message of hope for a better tomorrow?

Some people would answer "yes" to these last three questions. Influenced by dispensationalist thinking, there is no place in their eschatology for the concept of restoration or triumph for the Church in this age. They are persuaded that these endtimes will be an extended period of global catastrophe, social and moral disintegration, international upheaval, and individual trauma.

In contrast, today's apostles and prophets believe that this generation could be the one to see the fulfillment of Peter's declaration—made within days of Pentecost—that God will bring about a restoration of all things as was spoken of by the prophets, a restoration that will pave the way for the return of Jesus Christ from Heaven. For He "must remain in heaven *until*" this restoration is fully achieved (Acts 3:21).

Restoration Defined

In the general mind, the term *restoration* is most commonly associated with antique furniture or the renovation of old buildings to their original state. Unfortunately, the biblical concept of restoration has no such readily understood meaning. Henry Warner Bowden, past president of the American Society of Church History, said, "The meaning of the term *restoration* is relative to different people who appropriate it, to what *they* pursue under its aegis. Based on historical usage of institutional, doctrinal and biblical categories, there is no meaning intrinsic to the title, and we can find no common agreement on any set of organizational forms or ideas."[1]

But there are others who dispute Bowden's claim. For example, Theodore Dwight Bozeman, professor in the School of Religion and Department of History at the University of Iowa, contends that the Puritan period was characterized by restorationist thinking. He argued that the defining element of this thinking was a *"reversion...to the first, or primitive, order of things narrated in the Protestant Scriptures."*[2]

Bozeman's emphasis on the Puritan's restorationist ideal was a defining element with respect to current restorationist ideals. *Restorers* continue to seek (as they always have) to recover truth from the biblical record. *But they believe that to stop there would be far too limiting, for restoration is much more than recovering a primitive order or practice associated with the early Church.*

Richard Hughes, professor in the Religious Division at Perpperdine University, says, "If scholars are to use this concept [restoration] with creative dexterity,

1. Richard Hughes, ed., *The American Quest for the Primitive Church* (Chicago: University of Illinois Press, 1988), 2.

2. Theodore Dwight Bozeman, *To Live Ancient Lives: The Primitivist Dimension in New England Puritanism* (Chapel Hill: University of North Carolina Press, 1988), 11.

they must be less concerned with abstractions and generalizations and more concerned *with hearing how insiders—true believers in the restoration ideal—define the concept for themselves.*"[3]

In explaining this book's use of the term *restoration*, it is important to focus attention on Peter's great proclamation found in Acts 3:21:

He must remain in heaven until the time comes for God to restore everything, as He promised long ago through His holy prophets.

Peter clearly declares that restoration will do the following:

- Precede the return of Christ.

- See the fulfilling of all things prophesied by the prophets.

- Be the consummation of a process that has been going on over an extended period.

- Involve an element of *recovery*, but will be in itself *forward looking*, focused on the consummation of the age and the return of Christ.

It is a mistake to charge true "restorers" with being historical primitivists. *We do not seek to return to an original condition; rather, we seek to advance to the*

---

3. Hughes, *The American Quest*, 2.

*fullness of God's **original intention**.* Ours is not the backward look of nostalgia, hoping to find a dubious mythological perfection in the early Church. The Acts of the Apostles and the Epistles reveal that the primitive Church was hampered by schism, legalism, and licentious living, and it was infiltrated by the empty philosophies of the day. We have no desire for the future to be a repeat of such a past. Nevertheless, implicit in the letters of the apostles to the churches were strong moral and spiritual principles that are the life foundations of every authentic Christian community. It is these elements that modern-day restorers seek to recover as part of the process of advancing the Church to its fullness and maturity.

As Paul wrote to the Ephesian church, a full restoration of all ministries—apostle, prophet, evangelist, pastor, and teacher—must occur so that we can "...reach unity in the faith and in the knowledge of the Son of God and become mature, attaining to the whole measure of the fullness of Christ" (Eph. 4:13). God intends a post-denominational united Church to fill the world with His glory. That is why restoration must include *all* the ministry gifts.

Why Do Things Need Restoring?

When Jesus was confronted by the Pharisee on the question of divorce, He pointed out that Moses had introduced the bill of divorcement as a *concession* to them because of the hardness of their hearts. Then He went on to say, "But it was not this way from the beginning" (Mt. 19:8b). Jesus highlighted a divine principle that holds true in every issue of life. To discover the norm of God, we must first ask, "How was it in the beginning?" If we are to understand the *consummation* of the ages, we must first look not at the *post-fall condition* of man and our world, but at their *commencement*, at God's fully expressed *pre-fall intention* for man and this world.

The original progression of creation provides us with a clear understanding of the ultimate intentions of the Creator—intentions that figure strongly in the thinking of restorers today. They are as follows:

1. *God is the source of all creation* ("In the beginning God..." [Gen. 1:1]). This self-introduction provides no apologetic for the atheist, nor any evidential argument for the agnostic. God simply asserts the fact that He is the ultimate source, the first cause of all that has come into existence. There was nothing before or beyond Him. To the restorer, anything that cannot root itself in God as its source has no place in the life of the Christian or the practices of the community of God. Restoration, therefore, necessarily seeks to free the Church from all additions of human ritual, tradition, philosophy, and anything else that binds people with religious fetters or blinds them with religious darkness. Restoration demands a

return to God as the source, center, and sustainer of all things.

2. *Heaven and earth were originally in essential harmony with each other.* God created Heaven and earth. Although separate, distinct spheres, they were not mutually exclusive. God's will in Heaven was to find its expression in man's will on earth, which is why Jesus taught us to pray, "Your will be *done on earth as it is in heaven*" (Mt. 6:10b). Therefore, any culturally accepted practice that is not aligned with the righteousness and justice of God, such as homosexual practices, abortion, sexual relations outside of marriage, racism, cruelty, domestic violence, or unjust exploitation of the labor force, is both unacceptable and destined to pass away under God's judgment.

3. *Creation was an ordered process.* It was not a muddled jumble of everything brought into existence at once; rather, it was an ordered creation with God carrying out His plan according to a timetable— on the "first day" of the week, on the "second day" of the week, and so on. This is a continuing hallmark of authenticity in all God's working in our lives and in the corporate life of the Church. God is not the God of disjointed, random movement, but of orderly progress. Restoration is not a last-minute interventionist act that will conclude this age; it is a progressive process throughout time.

4. *Every act of creation was judged.* God's judgment is constructive in its intent, not destructive. God stood back from each act of His creation, surveyed it, and judged it "good." It is interesting to note that, *although God is perfect, He still judged what proceeded from His perfection.* In this way He affirmed that His creation was in keeping with His intention.

5. *Creation was diversity in perfect harmony.* Restorers do not think that the Church of God or the world around it should assume a bland and boring sameness. Restoration produces unity and harmony in the Body of Christ without destroying its rich diversity. *As the "restoration of all things" reaches its consummation, so Christ will manifest Himself more fully in the unified diversity of human culture.* The Kingdom of God is rich enough and wide enough to accommodate cultural diversity, as long as that diversity is not in itself an expression of unrighteousness or injustice.

6. *God's purpose remains unchanged.* When God created man, He delegated His authority to him to rule in the earth on His behalf. Man was created to be God's regent on earth. His mandate was to be fruitful, multiply, fill the earth, and rule (see Gen. 1:28 NAS). Had Adam and Eve never sinned and instead given themselves to fulfilling the will of God, then the earth would be filled with men and women in God's full

image and likeness. There wouldn't be anything on earth out of harmony with Heaven. Disease, sickness, poverty, pain, war, violence, greed, and all other consequences of sin would not have entered the human experience. *Restorers assert that although Adam fell, God's purpose did not change. God still intends a world totally compatible with Himself, one free of all that has come upon it as a consequence of the Fall.*

7. *God made the family the first unit of society.* When God made Adam, he was the only thing that God did not affirm as good. Adam was not flawed; rather, he was incomplete. God knew that essential to Adam's fulfillment was a partner with whom to share life. The creation of Eve was the completion of humanity, and the procreation of the first couple was the fulfillment of their union together and the beginning of "family." In these latter days, God's intention is to restore family relationships—including order and authority—so that the family is itself fulfilling and becomes the means through which society is fulfilled. This means that we can expect the recovery of family to exceed its original condition, which is also in keeping with God's original intention for it.

- *God will banish war and violence.* The world's increasing population was meant to become a regulated society of families, peoples, tribes, and nations covering the face of the earth. While maintaining their family relationships, God intended for people in general to be healed together by the common root in their father Adam. The thoughts of nations being formed by one people conquering another was never part of God's original intent. Therefore, in the restoration of all things, war will cease (see Is. 2:4).

- *People will find their fulfillment through accomplishing mission.* The mandate given to Adam provided him with a means of self-expression and fulfillment in doing the will of God; procreation and productive work were given to man *before the Fall.* God's purpose in providing work for people to do is to bestow on them the means by which they can express their creativity and enjoy the dignity of labor. Leisure is a *pleasurable* thing, but human beings find their *fulfillment* in work completed.

When Did God's Program of Restoration Begin?

Restoration was already in progress when man was created. In addition to the visible worlds of our universe, God had also created a world of invisible spirit beings, consisting of the angels, archangels, cherubim, and seraphim mentioned throughout the Scriptures. These beings were accorded rank and responsibility in the universal government of God.

Prisoners of Divine Purpose

(See Isaiah 6:2, Ezekiel 10:7, Matthew 18:10, First Timothy 5:21, and Jude 9.)

The most magnificent of these angelic beings was named Lucifer. He was described as "the model of perfection, full of wisdom and perfect in beauty" (Ezek. 28:12). Lucifer apparently mediated the worship of the universe before God's throne. God Himself ordained Lucifer to this position of responsibility:

You were anointed as a guardian cherub, for so I ordained you... (Ezekiel 28:14).

Through his God-given priestly role, Lucifer gained greater influence and respect. However, he abused his position and power by swaying some angels to join him in rebellion against the throne. He manipulatively used his position of honor and trust to seek independent authority and the personal worship of all creation.

Lucifer's plan to gain God's throne contained five different steps, each intended to increase his power and prominence. These steps are identified by the prophet Isaiah in the following passage:

How you have fallen from heaven, O morning star, son of the dawn! You have been cast down to the earth, you who once laid low the nations! You said in your heart, "I will ascend to heaven;

I will raise my throne above the stars of God; I will sit enthroned on the mount of assembly, on the utmost heights of the sacred mountain. I will ascend above the tops of the clouds; I will make myself like the Most High" (Isaiah 14:12-14).

1. "I will ascend." Lucifer's rebellion started from his place of God-given governmental authority. The earth then became the stage upon which the whole drama of rebellion, judgment, and restoration was enacted before the eyes of a watching universe. We can therefore understand the joy Jesus experienced in praying, "I have brought You glory on earth by completing the work You gave Me to do" (Jn. 17:4). God willed the scene of rebellion to witness the obedience of Christ, which paved the way for the restoration of all things to Himself, the utter banishment of evil from the universe, and the total destruction of Lucifer.

2. "I will raise my throne above the stars of God." The stars of God are symbolic of angelic beings. Lucifer despised his priestly office of mediating angelic worship. He was not satisfied with his place as "first among equals"; he wanted sovereign control over all other creatures. He wanted the angels to acknowledge his superiority over them; he wanted them to submit to his self-appointed lordship.

3. "I will sit enthroned on the mount of assembly." This phrase shows Lucifer's aspiration for cosmic supremacy. He coveted throne rule from which he could universally determine the course of events and have the right to issue decrees and laws. He saw himself as having supreme control over all things. Nothing would continue to exist apart from him.

4. "I will ascend above the tops of the clouds." In Scripture, the cloud frequently symbolizes the glory and presence of God (consider the cloud in the wilderness and on Mount Sinai [see Ex. 13:21-22; 19:16-20]). Lucifer wanted to be worshiped for every manifestation of his own nature and glory. He wanted this manifestation and worship to exceed that which God received.

5. "I will make myself like the Most High." The Most High is the possessor of heaven and earth (see Gen. 14:22 KJV). Thus Lucifer exposed his heart. Determined to possess all things, he desired ultimate ownership. Although a creature, he wanted to be the creator. Anything less was insufficient.

When God spoke the word of judgment against Lucifer's rebellion, Michael and the heavenly hosts moved swiftly against Lucifer and the angels that had joined him. The rebellious horde was driven from the mountain of God in disgrace. Expelled from God's presence, Lucifer forever lost his office as priest before the throne of God. His place in the government of God was finished. He was thrown down to earth where God would make a spectacle of him to all nations before his final dreadful end (see Ezek. 28:18-19).

The Earth Experiences Restoration

But all was not lost. The beginnings of restoration in the earth are found in the words "the Spirit of God was hovering over the waters" (Gen. 1:2b). These words brought hope for continued purpose in the earth. When God spoke and said, "Let there be light" (Gen. 1:3), a threefold interaction took place that began the process of restoration.

- *God's prophetic word* announced His intent to restore and called it into being;

- *God's Spirit*—personally attendant in readiness for something to happen—initiated the work of restoration;

- *God's divine power* was released, providing all that was needed to fully set in motion the restoration of all things.

This threefold interaction of Spirit, Word, and power is characteristic of every revival in history, and it is ever present in the process of restoration.

Prisoners of Divine Purpose

At the end of the first week of restoration, God crowned His action by creating man in His own image and likeness and proclaiming His intention for man to have the "rule" over all the rest of creation and to restore His government throughout the earth (see Gen. 1:26).

Lucifer must have shaken with rage at hearing these words of God. This other creature, this "Adam," created in the image of God, was immediately viewed by Lucifer as a rival. Seething with fury and frustration, he took counsel with his allies and plotted the fall of man. A further affront to Lucifer was his knowledge that this man was made "a little lower than the heavenly beings [angels]" (Ps. 8:5). To his distorted mind, God was demoting the status of his angelic rule and princedom. Not knowing the mind and ways of God, he could not conceive of the Most High planning to re-institute universal harmony and order through a man that was made lower than the angels. Far less could he conceive of man rising through obedience to occupy a position higher than that ever occupied by himself in his pre-fallen state. Man was destined for more than ministry before the throne; he was designed to ultimately share that throne (see Acts 7:56; Heb. 12:2; Rev. 3:21). Man is created to co-reign with Christ. Yet this is the result of his being *in Christ* through redemption, so that the supremacy of Christ is never in question.

God's intent for man incensed Lucifer, whose own aspiration and attempted usurpation of this position had incurred God's judgment upon himself. Now having observed man, who was created from dust, being given a place alongside God on His throne, Lucifer fumed with jealousy.

Meanwhile, the eyes of the whole universe were riveted on Adam. Creation was asking: Will this man be the means of universal restoration? Will he be able to subdue the rebellion at work in the cosmos? Will he bring Lucifer to his final, horrible end? Will he fill the earth with a people submitted to the government of God? Will he be the one to bring the whole structure of the universe back into alignment with the purpose of God?

The knowledge of such universal questions hardened Lucifer's resolve to destroy man, for his fallen mind had finally awakened to a new and awful prospect: *Man in the image of God was the key to God's restoring all things to their intended purpose.*

As the crown of God's creation, man did not evolve from some amoebic distortion in a primordial swamp, nor was he the random selection of a chance microscopic life form released by a great bang in the universe. It is inconceivable that the God of infinite intelligence and wisdom should—at the dawn of a creation sustained by incredibly complex and intricate systems of life support—choose some infantile, malformed, randomly selected, still-evolving creature to rule on His behalf! God chose man to rule everything else in order to supervise the return of everything to the fullness of its creation purpose. Man is, therefore, the key to the restoration purpose of God in all creative spheres, including the angelic orders, the cleansing of the heavens, the overthrow of satanic powers, and the establishment of righteousness and justice throughout the earth (see Ps. 8:4-6; 1 Cor. 6:3). The fact that Christ has assumed the highest place in the universe is indicative that, despite Adam's failure, it is still God's purpose that a God-man be universally supreme in all things (see Col. 1:18).

...In putting everything under [man], *God left nothing that is not subject to him. Yet at present we do not see everything subject to him. But we see Jesus, who was made a little lower than the angels, now crowned with glory and honor because He suffered death, so that by the grace of God He might taste death for everyone* (Hebrews 2:8-9).

Man's Role in Restoration

So God created man in His own image, in the image of God He created him; male and female He created them (Genesis 1:27).

The mandate given to Adam and Eve is a concise summation of the process of restoration, the process that God is using to bring everything into order. Within that order, everything advances toward its full creation intention. Adam and Eve's commission to rule was never a license for dictatorship or authoritarianism. Rather, it was designed to be the continued outworking of the father-heart of God—leading by example, governing by love—that would bring to fullness that which was still undeveloped or immature.

Man's guardianship extended to his environment. It is no coincidence that the nearer we come to the fullness of our age and the return of Jesus Christ, the more that environmental concerns have become major issues. Even in his warped and fallen condition, man still has an awareness of the divine commission. He realizes his responsibility for the environment and what he is doing to it, as well as for all the creatures dependent on that environment—including himself. The continued pollution of our world's rivers, waters, seas, and land; the increasing use of pesticides poisoning our soil; the endangering of the food chain; deforestation; genetically altered foods; and other ill-considered "advances" of genetic science—all these show the continued irresponsible attitude of fallen man toward his divine commission. Man may seek to hide his economic self-interests behind pseudo-moral motives, but the sum total of all that is happening in man's continued assault upon his environment is an abrogation of his mandate. There are consequences to flying in the face of divine purpose. Violation of God's mandate carries its own judgment.

When Adam—manifesting the divine image and likeness of God and operating as His regent with guardianship of the world and his fellow man—rebelled and fell, tragic consequences followed. As a result of Adam's sin there came alienation from God as well as domestic conflict, which led ultimately to violence and murder (see Gen. 4:1-8). Although man continued to exist after the Fall, he had entered into conflict with his creation purpose. He was now cut off from God, frequently at war with his fellow man, and at enmity with his world. Restoration, then, must incorporate the reconciliation of man to God, restoring fellowship between the Creator and His creature. It also must bring family reconciliation between man and man, as well as reconcile man to his responsibility as guardian of the earth and of his environment.

Chapter 3

God's Millennial Moment

WE MUST NOT enter the third millennium with blind faith. God wants us to have an informed faith. God sets no premium on ignorance. We must therefore understand our gospel. Let's start by asking ourselves the question, "Why did God create the universe?" The answer to this long-standing question provides the key to understanding *everything*—past, present, future, and on to the grand finale. The answer is found in John 3:35: "*The Father loves the Son and has placed everything in His hands.*" The universe is essentially the Father's love gift to His Son. *God's grand design throughout history is to bring Christ into possession of His inheritance, an inheritance that was His before it even existed!* Christ was God's appointed heir before creation ever took place. The decision to bring everything that Jesus would inherit into existence through Him displays the magnificent wonder of God's wisdom (see Col. 1:15-17). Through the Son, God brought into being all that the Son inherited, and through the Son, God created a people with whom the Son would share all things. God's people are joint heirs *in* Christ and *through* Christ (see Rom. 8:17).

Satan's hostility toward the Church stems from his root hostility toward God's divine purpose in giving His Son, Christ, the supreme authority over all things and our coming into Christ, which makes us His joint heirs. The conflict of the ages is the result of satan constantly seeking to overthrow Christ and the Church as heirs of all things. Remember, however, that *satan is not omniscient*; that attribute belongs to God alone. Unable to see into the future, satan is frustrated when, after initiating what he believes to be a superb plan, *he discovers that he has unwittingly served the purpose of God.* Nowhere is this more dramatically portrayed than in the cosmic conspiratorial alliance of satan—the combined powers of darkness and wicked men in the crucifixion of Christ. Following the resurrection, Peter announced that in crucifying Christ, wicked men had only done *what God had predetermined beforehand should be done* (see Acts 2:23). God continues to uphold this divine principle: He will protect all His children and make all things work together for the good of those who love Him (see Rom. 8:28).

But why allow satan to even assault God's people?

The present warfare between the Church and the powers of darkness is the means by which God is equipping and preparing His people for their place alongside Christ in the ruling of the universe in the ages to come. Through this conflict, God's people are learning to trust when they can't see; to submit and not to strive. Christ has already conquered sin and death completely, and the present work of the Spirit is manifesting that victory in the Church by its faith in the name of Christ as it engages and triumphs in spiritual warfare (see Eph. 6:12-13). It is through the hardships, challenges, and conflicts of life that our true measure as men and women becomes manifest. We are experiencing the conflict of this age intentionally. We are on probation, being proved and readied for our place alongside Christ in the age to come.

When Napoleon sought a seat in the French Chamber of Deputies (the equivalent to the British Parliament or U.S. Congress), men laughed and mocked him because of his youth. His reply to them was apt: "Men mature quickly on the battlefield, and, gentlemen, it is from the battlefield I have come." His response settled the issue and won his seat.

Triumph or Self-Destruction?

Dispensational pessimists depict the present evil age as being in the terminal stages of self-destruction. They hold out to us no other hope than the coming of Christ to rescue His people from the final death throes of humanity. According to them, Christ's coming will enact a rescue operation for the Church, which will be accomplished by snatching His beleaguered people away from the war zone. But how can we assert ourselves to be a triumphant Church if such is to be the conclusion of our time in this age? How can we claim that His enemies will become His footstool (see Acts 2:35) if this is to be the grand finale? How can we say, "Greater is He that is in us than he that is in the world" (see 1 Jn. 4:4 KJV), if this is the conclusion of the Church's testimony?

Conversely, many post-millennialists see a gradual Christianizing of the nations until the whole world and its structures become the Kingdom of God. They see apostasy and failure as things of the past. According to them, we are now moving into the ever-increasing light of the age to come.

Neither the optimist nor the pessimist is right. The Bible reveals that the moral values and lifestyle of the world, the structures of family life amongst unbelievers, and their economic security will continue to disintegrate (see 2 Tim. 3:1-7). The world will remain at enmity with God and under great pressure, and because of increasing evil, many Christians will fall away from the faith (see Mt. 24:12; 1 Tim. 4:1). But, as in the time of the early Church, progress will parallel persecution, and faith will explode in the hearts of ordinary people. The ruthless assault of satan upon the early Church was met by an outpouring of God's Spirit in revival power, with great miracles affirming Christ's resurrection and living presence. So it will be in our time as well (see Acts 2:17-21,39).

The apostle James prophesied of the end-time world harvest. Writing of the seasonal rains, he reminds us how the early rains enable farmers to plow and sow, while the latter rains come to swell the grain in preparation for the harvest. In these end-times we can expect comparable visitations of God (see Jas. 5:7-8). The refreshing moves of the Spirit on God's people will be great and widespread. The final, "grande finale" move of the Spirit will be of such proportions that multiplied thousands, possibly even millions, will be swept into the Kingdom of God. It will be a fulfillment of Amos' prophecy of the plowman being overtaken by the reaper (see Amos 9:13).

No sooner will the seed be in the ground than, by the miraculous influence of the Holy Spirit, there will be a speedy germination of the seed. It will put forth its shoot and roots, and it will come quickly to harvest. When this foretold harvest comes, seeing people confronted with the claims of the gospel and finding them ready to come into the Kingdom will not be a long, drawn-out affair; but rather, it will be a swift move of God. Christ is not coming to save a beleaguered Church from being overthrown, but for a triumphant Church that has overcome all its enemies, advanced His Kingdom across the earth, and reaped the greatest worldwide harvest of lost souls that the world has ever seen.

Christ declared to His followers:

I have given you authority to trample on snakes and scorpions and to overcome all the power of the enemy; nothing will harm you (Luke 10:19).

It is actually the risen Lord who is striding back and forth throughout His Body on earth, striking the forces of darkness with the two-edged sword of truth, driving them back, and chaining their influence among the nations through the transforming power of the gospel. Paul tells the Roman Christians, "The God of peace will soon crush Satan under your feet" (Rom. 16:20a). In folk religion, the posture of the Christian toward fallen angels is defensive: "*In Scripture the church is on the offensive, and the blows it receives from Satan come from a retreating enemy.*"[1]

---

1. Richard Lovelace, *The Dynamics of Spiritual Life* (Downers Grove, Illinois: InterVarsity Press, 1979), 136.

God's Millennial Moment

Although it is true that the biblical perspective of man in our world is that man has betrayed God's trust in the Garden; that the consequence of this betrayal was for man to be locked into a world apart from God; and that every effort on his part to control that world outside of Christ has demonstrated again and again his insufficiency, history shows that all progress of a righteous and just nature has only ever come about as a result of a divine visitation. This is not only in terms of spiritual revival, but also in God's own story—the heart and circumstance of man. History does not show major benefit of man's rule outside of Christ, but rather the failure of man's rule outside of Christ. But the prophetic view is not that that would continue until the end of the age, but that God would move powerfully in the end time to demonstrate His rule and authority through redeemed man.

We are not triumphalists, but we intend to triumph. Therefore, we must live and act accordingly. Tomorrow's age can be more and more our experience today as we increase our demonstration of God's values and standards in every area of our life and influence. We are not to leave everything to be sorted out in the future; we are to live the future now. Tomorrow telescopes back into today as we live in the light of the consummation of all things under the Lordship of Jesus Christ.

In 1978, Dr. Leighton Ford, then Chairman of the International Lausanne Committee for World Evangelisation, rightly said, "Other people can think about the future, worry about the future, plan for the future, fear the future, discuss the future. *But only God's people can live in the future.* We Christians live on the borderline of the 'already' and the 'not yet' of 'this age' and 'the age to come'. And that is because in Jesus Christ the future has already invaded time and grasped our lives."[2]

It is the new man—man of the *new order*, man *in Christ*—who holds the key to the restoration of all things that is spoken of by the prophets. What kind of people are these people of the new order? They are just like the Man who has already achieved the throne rule: They are *like Christ*, for they are *in Christ*.

2. Donald E. Hoke, ed., *Evangelicals Face the Future* (South Pasadena, California: William Carey Library, 1978), 41.

Chapter 4

One Around the Throne

Restoring the Radical Edge

WE ARE TO BE "like Christ," but what does that really mean?

Someone once said that Jesus "put a face on God" by coming among people and touching, lifting, embracing, and caring for them in their hurts and needs. As we embrace Christ's radical mission, recognizing that the Father sends us even as He sent Jesus (see Jn. 20:21), then we too wear the face of God in our generation. It's still God's intention to walk into our cities, towns, and rural areas and touch and lift the fallen, broken, hurting, and dying of humanity. We must refuse to become hardened to the needs around us if we are to avoid becoming a Church *having form without power* (see 2 Tim. 3:5).

As the "future Church," we need to strip ourselves of any unacceptable religious layers that are obscuring God's love for people. This is imperative, for we are faced with a generation that has little idea of who Jesus is. Most unbelievers see the Christ that the Church portrays as being so gentlemanly in behavior and attitude—wanting to be at peace with everyone and to please all—that Jesus the revolutionary teacher, the controversial prophet, the passionate preacher, and the implacable opponent of religious hypocrisy has disappeared from view. As the late Anglican Archbishop William Temple once remarked, "*Why any man should have troubled to crucify the Christ of liberal Protestantism has always been a mystery.*"[1]

In reality Christ, the supreme restorer, was the most radical Man who ever walked the earth. The people of His day recognized an authority in His teaching, an authority previously unseen (see Mt. 7:29). He was the first of a new order of mankind. His incisive and unapologetic preaching concerning the demands of the Kingdom of God incensed the Pharisees, Saduccees, lawyers, and other representatives of the power structures of His time.

---

1. William Temple, *Readings in St. John's Gospel* (New York: MacMillan Press, 1942), xxix.

When Christ entered the temple at the commencement of His ministry and found the outer courts turned into a marketplace, He wasn't just a little "put out" by the fact that the Gentiles had been expelled from the area that God designated as a place of prayer for Gentiles (all nations). He did not say to Himself, "Oh, I must report this offense so that it can be discussed at the next temple business meeting." No, Jesus exploded with fiery, prophetic passion and drove the merchandisers out with a whip of cords (see Jn. 2:15). He confronted hypocrisy head-on while warning His disciples against its insidious creeping deception (see Lk. 12:1).

Jesus constantly challenged attitudes that obscured the heart of God, and in the process, He forced legalists to show themselves for what they were. Walking with His disciples through the cornfields on the Sabbath, knowing that they would eat from the corn (see Lk. 6:1); healing on the Sabbath day with full knowledge that it would offend the priests (see Mt. 12:11-12); prophesying the destruction of the temple from its own steps and then speaking of rebuilding it in three days, knowing that they would not understand that He was speaking of His own body in death and resurrection (see Mt. 26:61)—all these provocative actions were undertaken with the full awareness that they would provoke angry, inflexible, legalistic responses from the religious hierarchy.

What is our response to religious legalism and hypocrisy in the Church today? How much longer will we tolerate the intolerable, support the insupportable, and negotiate the non-negotiable? Should we blindly and unquestioningly continue to do this? How much longer will we continue to financially support self-declared homosexuals as bishops and priests in churches? How long will we continue to entrust our money to churches with investments in the arms industry or in corporations exploiting "cheap" labor in Third World countries? How long will we salary priests who deny the virgin birth or resurrection of Jesus Christ? Is it not time for passionate prophetic confrontation again?

Jesus calls us to embrace a radical lifestyle and to follow Him as true children of the Kingdom. On meeting the rich young ruler who "trusted in his riches," He demanded that the man sell everything and give the money to the poor (see Mt. 19:16-26; Lk. 18:18-27). The problem was not simply that the man possessed wealth. Rather Jesus saw that the man's wealth possessed him. By confronting this young man in this way, Jesus was saying to him, "Am I sufficient for you? If everything else was gone, would you be content in your relationship with Me, or am I merely one more among your many possessions?" His is a call to radical discipleship, to submission to Christ as He breaks the hold of materialism on you. The pursuit of money and other material things frequently sears the conscience, undermines intentions, blunts testimony, and neutralizes zeal. We are to be *stewards*, not *slaves* of possessions. It does not matter that Paul said that the world is "passing away" (1 Cor. 7:31). Our eyes are fixed beyond the material for "the prize of the high calling of God in Christ Jesus" (Phil. 3:14 KJV).

Jesus' radical actions were not moments of human weakness or intolerance, but expressions of God's heart. Radical Christianity will always be passionate, jealous as well as zealous, and white-hot for the divine interests involved.

Let me be clear: Deliberately disruptive, contentious, odd, or anarchistic behavior is not being radical. The message of restoration is radical in the sense that *it goes to the roots or the fundamentals of an issue.* When used in this sense, *non-radical Christianity is a contradiction in terms.* The thrust of the Spirit in our time is in prompting the Church to return to its roots in order to go forward to God's ultimate intention.

It is radical to pursue the genuine objective of rediscovering our true foundations—the bedrock of our conviction of faith in Christ—and to uncompromisingly advance from there until we overcome every obstacle in our way. We must destroy the wrong mental images we have of God and retrain our minds to think correctly about Him. He is not dour, angry, or quick to judge, but neither is He a genial, smiling Santa Claus in the heavens. *He is as Christ is. To see Christ is to see the Father.* Jesus "brought" the invisible God into visible being.

What About Our Traditions?

When *restorers* say it is important to discard *traditions* to rediscover authentic Christianity, we must clarify what tradition we are talking about. The word *tradition* literally means to "hand on," and it is used in its broadest sense to describe the process by which the faith is "handed on" to each new generation. Prayer for the sick, laying on of hands, anointing with oil, the Eucharist, and baptism *are all biblical traditions essential to the understanding, practice, and outworking of authentic Christianity.* In this sense, we refer to them collectively as the Tradition (upper case). Paul uses the word *tradition* in this sense when referring to the Eucharist as he handed *on what he had received as an essential element of the gospel* (see 1 Cor. 11:23).

Other traditions (lower case) are customary ways that different groups have of doing things, which are often peculiar to themselves. These are not part of the Tradition and should not be imposed upon other Christians or groups—for example, various expressive ways of worship, dancing, clapping, etc., or the celebration of special days that are meaningful for a particular church but not necessarily for others. These traditions should be examined in the light of Scripture. Restorers call for keeping Tradition and reexamining all lesser traditions as to whether they should be continued or discarded. This is nowhere better expressed than by Richard P. McBrien, who said, "If a tradition cannot be rejected or lost without essential distortion of the gospel, it is part of Tradition itself. If a tradition is not essential (i.e. if it does not appear, for example, in the New Testament, or if it is not clearly taught as essential to Christian faith), then it is subject to change or even elimination."[2]

Radical Politics

People sometimes ask, "Should the Church meddle in political issues?" The fact that politics is about the use of power over people means that the Church is *already* involved. Politics affects people, which makes it an issue for the Church.

The question is not whether we as Christians should or should not be involved with politics. Rather, we must ascertain which issues we should be most concerned with and what the wisest course of action for expressing our convictions in these matters may be.

---

2. R.P. McBrien, *CATHOLICISM Study Edition* (Minneapolis, Minnesota: Winston Press, 1981), 66.

We really identify well with John Neuhaus, who said, "To build a world in which the strong are just, and power is tempered by mercy, in which the weak are nurtured and the marginal embraced, and those at the entrance gates and those at the exit gates of life are protected by both law and love."[3] This is our hope, our long-term objective in life.

However, we also know that the working of the Spirit goes deeper than the reformation of political agendas or society and its institutions. God's purpose goes to the very transformation of the heart of man. The radical gospel recognizes the fact that the cultural lifestyle of society is the consequence of the corporate action and convictions of man. That is why restoration calls for *righteousness and justice* in public life.

Although I have stated that being radical should not be seen as being synonymous with social rebellion, that does not mean that we are to isolate ourselves from the socio-political debates on race, homelessness, abortion, gender, genetic engineering, and the many other issues of our day. We recognize that the fundamental nature of our gospel will not allow us to be escapists; rather, it demands that

3. James M. Boice, ed., "The Christian and the Church," *Transforming Our World* (Portland, Oregon: Multnomah, 1988), 120.

we be radically involved in our times. Gordon Mac-Donald said, "For almost 70 or 80 years, the consistent typical preaching from our pulpits has been eschatological and prophetic, and we have trained our people to think 'bail out' and to avoid serious responsibility for the world in which we live."[4] It has not greatly changed since Gordon MacDonald said those words. We must change our thinking in this area. Escapism is never an option; Jesus showed us that through His life and preaching. God demands involvement. The cross is the ultimate proof of God's involvement.

An example of being radical in the right way is in our response to poverty. Being radical does not mean that we abandon all wealth in order to identify with the poor or oppressed. *Becoming impoverished does not help the poor.* Scripture tells us that poverty is like a bandit and that the poor are vulnerable to oppression (see Prov. 6:11; Eccles. 5:8). Let's reject the sentimentality that gives rise to hypocritical middle class clichés that speak of the "blessing" of poverty. It's a curse—ask anyone who is poor. Instead, let's work together to set the poor free. Why imprison ourselves in the chains of poverty when we need to be free to deliver the poor from theirs? *We are radical when we actively address the root causes of people's poverty and*

---

4. Donald E. Hoke, ed., *Evangelicals Face the Future* (South Pasadena, California: William Carey Library, 1978), 86.

prophetically confront the powers that enslave. There is no need for the poor to remain poor in our present world. It is the lack of compassion, as well as injustice, international self-interest, encouragement of debt, and other factors that keep people trapped in their poverty. The Christian community must be different and prophetically challenge our world. That will possibly mean incurring the wrath of the very oppressors from which we seek to liberate others.

How Drastic Must the Changes Be?

The paradigms of most things are changing in this generation because they are no longer sufficient for what presently is, or for what is coming. We must escape the ruts of settling for the average, of accepting conventional wisdom, and of falling prey to "group think." *We must do more than merely **think of changing;** we must **change our way of thinking**.* The changes that God's people face are not cosmetic ones; they are fundamental, and they will consequently prove much more disruptive than merely altering programs, styles, or objectives. This is why many people in historic/traditional denominations get angry. They see the proclamation of God's radical Church as a frontal assault upon the denominational or non-denominational Church that they love and have grown up in. They do not want things to change; they want things to remain as they have always been.

But change is an absolute necessity in our historic time frame. God has said that in the last days He will shake all things—and this with the intention that only the unshakable will be able to stand. Having said this, He immediately announces what it is that will survive the end-time shaking, namely, *the Kingdom of God* (see Heb. 12:26-27). The Kingdom of God is not merely a teaching, a theology, or a phrase; it is the present dynamic reality of God's rule in this time/space world. Consequently, life in the Kingdom of God is a radical experience.

We are being radical when the following are true in our lives:

- *We embrace the gospel* that joins us to others and their needs and that cuts us free from the destructive influence of our independent self-will (see Rom. 12:4-5).

- *We embrace the consequences* of following His direction and Spirit regardless of what those consequences prove to be. This frees us from self-preservation and the fear of death (see Acts 4:18-19).

- *We maintain a pioneering attitude* rather than settling in self-comfort zones; we are pilgrims, not settlers (see Heb. 11:13-16).

- *We live free* of the slavish domination of the material and the temporal. Money can enslave;

decisions, actions, directions, relationships, and even ministry can be controlled by the desire for the temporal or for money (see 1 Tim. 6:10).

- *We confidently confront* the powers of darkness that oppose us rather than allow them to paralyze us in fear (see Mk. 16:17-18).

- *We do not wait for others* to do what we can and should do for ourselves. It is not for us to wait for something to be done by others; rather it is for us to make it happen (see Gal. 6:5).

- *We refuse to compromise* the truth to accommodate religious externalism or to protect any position or status we may have gained (see Acts 4:18-19).

- *We remain resolutely committed* to Christ as Head of the Church and refuse to fossilize in religious institutionalism (see Gal. 5:1; Col. 1:18).

- *We live by faith* finding our security in God's faithfulness to His Word rather than in what we see. It is in this way that we experience the law of the Spirit: "Man does not live on bread alone, but on every word that comes from the mouth of God" (Mt. 4:4b).

Isaiah presents the word of God as a living, active power package. When God's word leaves His mouth, it begins a purposeful "round-trip" journey, and God will not allow it to return until it has accomplished the purpose for which it was sent (see Is. 55:11). Every believer can be secure in this knowledge: If a word has been received from God, a word concerning family life, social relationships, ministry, church, health, finances, present, future—*whatever*—if that word has not yet come about, *it still remains in force. God will not allow His word to terminate short of its purpose.*

As *restorers* we are called to live out a vision, not to live in a dream. *The radical message of restoration is a call to stand in the liberty that we have received in Christ.* Isaiah's prophecy concerning Jerusalem in the last days was that she would rise up, shake the dust from her garments, and release herself from the yoke round her neck. In other words, she was to take radical action on her own behalf (see Is. 52:1-2). We must throw off the chains of false prophecies as well as our own past wrongs and mistakes for which we've repented and found forgiveness. We must pursue the fullness of God's purpose for our lives.

Tomorrow's world will be ruled by the radical men and women of today's world, who live, as their spiritual forefathers did, in the light of God's purpose.

Locked Into the Past or Liberating the Future?

Whenever a new move of the Spirit brings revelation to the Body of Christ, there are always voices raised in opposition, "prophesying" that it will eventually amount to little, since (they say) that is what has happened historically throughout previous generations.

As an organized movement, Pharisaism is traceable to the Maccabean period, but according to some scholars, it actually began as a restorationist movement in the days of the prophet Ezra. It was born in a season of revival as Israel returned to the land after 70 years of captivity in Babylon. The early Pharisees were zealous to continue Ezra's work of restoring the Word of God to a central place in the life and experience of Israel, and they were committed to purging Israel of all the evil practices espoused while in captivity. However, in process of time, their commitment gave way to hypocritical externalism and a legalistic bondage to the letter of the law. This bondage to the letter of the law so blinded them to its message that some of them were among the prime motivators in having Jesus killed.

In 2,000 years of history since Christ, this tragedy has been repeated many times. The revival movement of one generation will perceive itself as threatened by the "new thing," and in fear of being undermined or overtaken, the members of the past movement will oppose God's visitation on this new generation. *A thing only remains "new" if it continues to express new life that springs from the heart.*

Jesus spoke of the necessity of keeping new wine in new wineskins to show the need for *continuing flexibility.* This message was not about a new experience of the Holy Spirit, one that expressed itself in new songs and ways in the congregation. A close examination of the passage reveals that Jesus was responding to a question about why His disciples were not fasting. His response *likened the disciples to new wine,* which must not be poured into old wineskins. He was saying, in effect, that *they must not allow themselves to become molded and hardened into old patterns, forms, and expressions of external, religious life* (see Mk. 2:18-22).

We are already being poured into old wineskins if our concerns are locked into refining, redefining, restating, and protecting what we already have instead of continuing to progress toward what lies before us. As the new wine of God, we must not allow the expectations and intimidation of others to pour us into old religious patterns and forms. We are not called to conform to the old but to advance in the new. *Restoration is only restoration if it **continues** to restore. Religious externalism is a terminal practice; its forms, methods, and practices are merely the death throes of that which was once vibrant with life.*

As we enter the third millennium, there is now a great possibility that everything will take a new shape in this generation. It will be nearer to what God is after than ever before: Christ in power in the streets of life, in peoples' homes, and in the workplace, with the miracle of God's transforming power healing the minds and bodies of men and women. Hundreds of thousands around the world will turn to Christ *outside* of the exclusive context of religious buildings and meetings. The main Church concerns will not be the building program, mission development, music ministry, etc.; rather, it will be the power of God manifest among His people. His Spirit and Word will meet the people's deep longing for spirituality. The people of God will no longer criticize or compete with each other, but unified in love, they will continue to move toward maturity as apostles, prophets, and teachers live and minister amongst them.

The Cry for Unity

Whether it wants to or not, everything in history is moving toward unification in Christ. The purpose of this ultimate fullness will continue to unfold in the age to come. However, having tasted of the powers of the age to come, we should be manifesting the ultimate unification in Christ in this present age. The cosmic order of *the age to come is the life of the Spirit, infusing and ordering the life of God's people today*. The manifestation of the unity of human society, longed for among the nations and foretold by the prophets, is that to which the Church is called now (see Jn. 17:21).

Throughout successive generations, testimony to the continuing desire for unity has run like a deep river of hope within the heart of the Christian Church. Burdened voices have been raised in prophetic intercession for the working of God's Spirit to bring His people to unity. Richard Baxter, an outstanding Puritan pastor, wrote, "No part of my prayers are so deeply serious as that for the conversion of the infidel and ungodly world….[and] *except the case of the infidel world, nothing is so sad and grievous to my thoughts as the case of the divided churches….*"[5]

The *restorer's* radical message and stance angers those with vested interest in the status quo or those desiring the continuation of their undisturbed comfort zones. Many claim that pursuing the unity of the Church is at best wishful thinking and at worst a devious ploy calculated to cause further division of the Body by drawing people out of the traditional historical denominations and into obscure restorationist cults. They strongly assert that true unity can come about only *after* the return of Christ, and they vigorously claim that history itself is against this

5. J. van den Burg, *Constrained by Jesus Love* (Kampen: H. Kok N.V., 1956), 27.

unity occurring this side of Christ's return. *If this is true, then we must inevitably conclude the following things:*

- *History is sovereign.* God is no longer God over all, but God is subject to the inevitability of history. Therefore, history ultimately reigns.

- *Jesus' prayer for the Church to be one will remain unfulfilled.* This will have dire consequences, for Jesus plainly stated that the unity of the Church would be the trigger for the world to believe (see Jn. 17:21-22). If unity can come only after His return, then it will be too late for the world to believe, for His return will be to bring judgment to the world and not a new opportunity for salvation (see Jude 14-15).

- *There will be no triumphant Church to greet the Lord at His coming.* Instead, there would be a beleaguered remnant of surviving believers, defeated and divided, waiting to be rescued and suddenly transformed into perfection by the power of Christ in His coming.

- *Christ's Bride, the Church, will not be ready for the wedding supper,* since she will still be clothed in garments spotted by the world.

- *The unity of the faith will not have been attained,* and the fullness of Christ will remain out of reach.

- *The "restoration" of all things spoken by the prophets will have been thwarted.* This would lay God open to the charge of either not having told the truth or not keeping His word.

Such a consummation to this age is both unbiblical and unthinkable. Restorers believe that the purpose of God will succeed, that Christ is greater than history, that the unifying power of His Spirit is greater than any divisions between men, and that the power of His resurrection life in the Church is greater than the combined powers of darkness raging against it through the structures of men. Having said this, we do not believe unity is found by ignoring our differences or by pretending that we are one by fellowshipping on the lowest common denominator of agreement.

Some years ago I was a member of a ministerial fellowship chaired by a prominent evangelical pastor in the city. He was under stress because of the significant growth of our church. His church had been the largest in the city, but ours had bypassed it in congregational size. He began denouncing us from the pulpit. Finally, I asked that we meet to discuss the problem, but he refused point-blank. Yet at the next ministerial fellowship meeting, he proposed inviting an internationally renowned evangelical evangelist to hold a citywide crusade, and he asked that we all "*show our unity*" by cooperating together in this program. When my associate raised the question,

"Should we not first face our divisions?" This pastor lost his composure and launched into a highly emotional tirade, which accused us of being divisive if we would not cooperate with his program!

It's time to get real! Unity requires that we face our difficulties and divisions in a forthright manner and dealing with them in a mature way. As someone once said, "We'd better grow up before we grow old!" We should not remain paralyzed by fear of what is involved or what might happen, nor should we be intimidated by those in power positions who are seeking to hold on to the status quo. Let's talk, pray, and start person-to-person, one-on-one, church-with-church, until the wisdom of God manifests itself and reconciles the seemingly irreconcilable.

Is unity possible? I believe that the key to achieving it lies with the emergence of apostolic ministries and teams, which we shall examine in more detail later in this book. It is time to make a strong advance in the area of unity by finding our God-designed place, networking within the Body of Christ, and walking in covenant, support, and security with the churches and people of God.

Chapter 5

Kingdom of God: The Invisible Presence

A S A YOUNG PREACHER, I was once invited to speak in both the morning and evening services at a small church in my hometown. However, following the morning meeting, I was hurriedly taken into the vestry and informed by the board of elders that I would not be required for services that evening due to my "erroneous" views concerning the Kingdom of God.

That morning, I had preached that we do not wait until after death or the rapture to enter the Kingdom; rather, the Kingdom was already expressed *in this age* with the coming of Christ and in the subsequent outpouring of the Spirit on God's people. The elders of this church, locked into the idea that Heaven and the Kingdom of God were essentially one and the same, were convinced that we enter both only after death or the rapture.

This episode highlights some of the confused thinking surrounding the Kingdom of God. Some of this confusion is because the Bible speaks of the Kingdom in a paradoxical manner. It portrays the Kingdom as a present reality (see Mt. 12:28; 21:31; Lk. 11:20; 17:21), and yet we are also told to pray for it to come (see Mt. 6:10; Lk. 11:2). Those who are born again of God's Spirit have already entered it (see Jn. 3:5). However, one day we will also be invited to enter it (see Mt. 25:34; 2 Pet. 1:11). Only through understanding the biblical usage of the term *Kingdom of God* can we solve these seeming contradictions.

The Kingdom of God can be best defined as "the rule of God in action." To be in the Kingdom of God is to be under God's active rule; hence, even Jesus—the King of kings—established His Kingdom through perfect submission to His Father. Although there is equality within the Godhead, the Son does not strive to find it (see Phil. 2:6), and there is an established governmental order in the function of Father, Son, and Holy Spirit (see 1 Cor. 15:25-28).

Kingdom of God: The Invisible Presence

The Kingdom of God and Heaven are not inter-changeable concepts, nor is the Kingdom and the Church. The Kingdom of God existed before the Church came into being, for the rule of God was already established in the heavens and the earth (see Ps. 103:19). The Church is the agent of the Kingdom in the sense that it is in and through the Church that the Kingdom of God is made evident and that the rule of God is manifested. This is not because we *claim* to be in the Kingdom or *talk about* being in the Kingdom or even *preach about* being in the King-dom; it is because we experience the righteousness, peace, and joy of being in the Kingdom (see Rom. 14:17).

On entering the Kingdom of God, the Spirit moves into action to establish the rule of God in our *soul*, which includes *the mind, emotions*, and *will*. The soul has always been the arena of greatest internal conflict. For us to believe that the total soul of a man can be established under the rule of the Kingdom is to confess we believe that sanctification can purify the soul.

This conflict expresses itself first in the arena of our minds, as we grapple with the truths of God as they are presented to us. The Kingdom of God col-lides head-on with the rationalistic thought process-es of modern man, demanding a transformation of the mind. Now that we are redeemed, the work of the

Holy Spirit in sanctification takes us through the process of establishing our thoughts, ideas, and plans under God's rule in His Word. The more the mind proves to be obedient to the Spirit, the more we will see and confess that we have the mind of Christ (see 1 Cor. 2:16).

We can say that this is equally true of our emotions. God has again and again shown the importance of having our emotions under His rule. There are several illustrations in the lives of men throughout the Bible that demonstrate the consequences of unruled emotions getting the better of a person (e.g., David and Bathsheba in Second Samuel 11:2-5, Demas and this present evil age in Second Timothy 4:10, etc.). These illustrations show the devastating power of unruled emotions in bringing destruction to a person. However, when God's Kingdom enters the soul, He transforms our godless lusts and passions into passionate and shameless love for Him.

The process of the Kingdom of God taking reign over our souls finds its fiercest battle in the arena of our wills. The Kingdom of God finds true expression in man's total submission to the will of God. Jesus put it this way, "Your kingdom come, Your will be done..." (Mt. 6:10). When our wills come under total domination of the will of the Father, then we can truly say, "The Kingdom has come!"

The Kingdom and Israel

In the minds of Jews in Jesus' day was great Kingdom expectation. The Jews anticipated the coming of the Messiah, the legitimate son of David; they looked for His coming to occupy His throne. It was believed that the Messiah, in ushering in God's Kingdom, would crush all opposition to God's will, destroy Israel's enemies, and set up His Kingdom rule in the midst of the nation. They believed that the whole affair would be highly visible, tangible, and material. Sadly, the majority failed to recognize Jesus as their Messiah and King (see Acts 13:27). They failed to seize God's moment (see Lk. 19:44).

The Kingdom of God is not *religious* in the sense that it represents a body of liturgy, form, and practice. Neither is it *geographical*, confined to the "holy land" of historical or present-day Israel. It is not political, as it is not a democratic or socialistic state; nor is it a dictatorship. The Kingdom of God is not nationalistic since it encompasses all nations, colors, and languages. It is not sexist because it embraces both male and female. And it is not racist, for it welcomes Jew and Gentile alike. *It is God's proactive rule in every sphere.*

The Kingdom of God was right before the eyes of Israel, but they did not have the spiritual perception to recognize it. The Jews' theology had ruined them for their time of visitation. When the Pharisees asked Jesus to tell them when the Kingdom of God would come, He told them that it would not come with careful observation, nor in a way in which people could say, "Here it is." Rather, He declared that the Kingdom of God would be within (see Lk. 17:20-21). This went beyond their ability to spiritually understand the implications of His words.

The unrest in the Middle East continues, and whenever restorers mention Israel, they stir up a hornets' nest. A few years ago, a series of articles entitled "The Truth About Israel" appeared in our magazine, *Restoration*. Within weeks we had letters from all over the world, were contacted by Jewish organizations and supporters from several countries, found ourselves the center of attention in many Christian and non-Christian magazines, and were featured in several issues of the *Jerusalem Post*. The correspondence and articles demonstrated that intense polarization still exists among many people with regard to Israel. In fact, Israel remains one of the most divisive issues facing evangelical Christianity today. For one man, the nation of Israel can do no wrong; for others, she can do no right. Restorers refuse to be pigeonholed in either extreme, though, because neither is correct.

Following the flood in Noah's time and God's judgment on the world at Babel, God turned from dealing with mankind as a whole and focused on a man whom He could trust—Abram. God called Abram, knowing that he would respond and base his life on God's direction. Abram was to be the man to introduce the seed of the new world order—the Kingdom of God.

It is important to note that Abram was counted as righteous *before* he was circumcised, not after. This fact alone shows that our justification before God and our receipt of His promises are by faith and not by works. Since Abraham was justified while uncircumcised, then the covenant promises are not exclusive to those who are circumcised, that is, the Jews. Circumcision was a *sign* of God's covenant, not the *basis* for it. This also means that Abraham is the father of all who believe. *Consequently, those who remain unbelievers, whether Jew or Gentile, are excluded from the covenant promises.* Jew and Gentile are received as one in Christ and are Abraham's seed on the basis of faith.

Although restorers fully accept that God's plan of salvation came first to Israel, they also assert that His plan was always intended to include the rest of the world. God's intention from the beginning was much larger than natural Israel (see Is. 49:6).

Genealogically, Jesus is rooted into both Abraham and David. He is described as not just descended from, but as being the Son of David and *the* Son of

Abraham. This means that He is *the* one whom God was specifically referring to when telling David that his seed would succeed him...and that God would establish the throne of his kingdom forever. Additionally, Jesus is the Seed promised to Abraham through which God would bless the whole world.

Restorers, therefore, see the hope of Israel and the gospel of Christ *as two phases of the same purpose* of Almighty God. The hope of Israel is the promise made to the fathers, which finds its fulfillment in Jesus Christ. I want to be very clear here. It isn't that God, disappointed with Israel, introduced a replacement theology by discarding Israel and taking up with the Church; rather, *Israel and the Gentiles were both a part of God's restoration plan from the beginning.*

In the time of Jesus, the Jews laid claim to being the people of God through their ancestral roots in Abraham. Through John the Baptist, God spoke directly to the nation about its self-righteous claim, warning them that *they shouldn't think of themselves as the children of Abraham if they weren't displaying the faith of Abraham.* As John declared, God was well able to raise up children to Abraham from the stones (see Mt. 3:9-10). At that time, God's judgment was already poised to strike at the root of the nation because of its lack of fruit in righteousness and faith.

Kingdom of God: The Invisible Presence

God rejected the Jews' claim to being the people of God on the basis of natural ancestry. He declared that the sons of Abraham, the true Jews, are those born of faith and circumcised in their hearts. This did not mean that Jesus was anti-Semitic. Rather, the Jews could no longer trust in a natural heritage because *true sonship of Abraham is not an issue of race, but of faith.* Jesus declared this very strongly when some Pharisees arrogantly boasted about being Abraham's seed. He wiped out their claim and exposed them as children of the devil because of their persistent and intransigent unbelief (see Jn. 8:39-51). He later sealed their fate by saying that the Kingdom of God would be taken from them and given to others who would produce its fruit (see Mt. 21:42-44).

The gospel is first to the Jews, God's natural children, and then to the Gentiles, His children by adoption. We should expect that many would rise up with passion to preach the gospel to the Jewish people. As Gentiles, we cannot take an elitist position toward Israel. Paul encouraged the church at Rome to not boast or be arrogant about their newfound place in the purposes of God (see Rom. 11:18-21).

Through the blood of Jesus, the dividing wall of hostility is broken down, and the law of commandments and regulations is abolished so that, together, both Jew and Gentile will be able to co-labor and co-partner in the House of God (see Eph. 3:6).

Paul brought us understanding of what happened to Israel by explaining that it was a mystery that had now been revealed to God's apostles and prophets: Israel's fall and setting aside was not God's *breaking covenant*, but His *keeping covenant* with Israel. In calling the Gentiles to Himself, God was keeping covenant with Israel. What has happened to natural Israel is temporary. Once God has drawn into Christ the full number of the Gentiles, Israel will experience a spiritual awakening and be grafted in again. Israel's restoration will be on such a scale that Scripture likens it to resurrection from the dead, and it will lead to major worldwide harvest. However, Paul did not teach that the return of Christ would trigger this awakening and harvest, as many believe. Rather, it is the fullness of the Gentiles that triggers the Spirit's moving out to Zion (see Rom. 11:11-15,25-26). When the complete number of Gentiles has been redeemed, then God will move quickly to save the Jews. This worldwide spiritual awakening will precede the return of Christ.

The Kingdom and the Arab Nations

Charismatic and evangelical Christians must face up to the fact that unquestioned support for Israel and persistent denunciation of Arabs in the Middle East does not serve the purpose of God. Our Arab Christian brothers—who are far more numerous than our Jewish Christian brothers—feel deeply hurt when fellow Christians behave toward them as though Christ had never truly liberated them. They see the way that many Christians give unqualified support to Israel without considering issues of justice as being more akin to Old Covenant understanding than New Covenant realities.

Although God's promise to Abraham and Sarah was to be fulfilled in her bearing the child of promise, Abraham's heart nevertheless was strongly knit with his son Ishmael, the result of his union with Hagar. Abraham knew from God's covenant promises that Isaac's future was secure—that he would be blessed and be a blessing—but the ache in Abraham's heart caused him to cry out in the wilderness, "If only Ishmael might live under Your blessing!" (Gen. 17:18b) God's immediate response to Abraham was not only to affirm His covenant with Isaac, but also to confirm His continued care and concern for Ishmael. God said, "And as for Ishmael, I have heard you: I will surely bless him; I will make him fruitful and will greatly increase his numbers. He will be the father of twelve rulers, and I will make him into a great nation" (Gen. 17:20).

Ishmael was 13 years old at this time, and both he and his father Abraham were circumcised that very same day, along with all the men servants of the house. Side by side, the 99-year-old father with his

13-year-old son received by faith the covenant seal of circumcision before God.

Christians know who the descendants of Isaac are, but they often ask, "Who are the descendants of Ishmael?" These are the present-day Arabs, the majority of whom are Muslim and proudly claim Abraham as their father. Almost 2 out of 11 people in our world today is Muslim. No longer confined to the Middle East, they have spread throughout all continents. Islamic fundamentalism has been the source of world attention in recent years with major revolutions taking place in nominal Arab states. As a consequence, Christians tend to view all Arabs as dangerous, if not fanatical Muslims, which is not true. We should be asserting in prayer that God is faithful to every promise that He has made, including those made to Ishmael initially and, subsequently, to Arab nations.

Restorers strongly assert that not only has God promised an extensive and speedy spiritual awakening in Israel (see Is. 66:8), but that He has equally promised that the Arab world will turn to Christ as well. Our hope is well beyond a limited visitation on the nation of Israel; it extends right across the Middle East. The *domination of Islam will be broken* by the love and power of God, and former enemies will be reconciled through their common faith in Christ. As a result of this newfound unity, there will come world blessing. Israel, Egypt, and Assyria (Syria, Iraq, Kuwait, and Jordan) will all worship together and become part of God's worldwide army of Spirit-anointed evangelists (see Is. 19:19-25). God has promised, and in faithfulness, He will fulfill these prophetic promises before the return of Jesus Christ (see Acts 3:21). These former Islamic nations will become Charismatic nations in spreading the gospel evangelistically.

In Christ, the great conflict between the kingdom of darkness and the Kingdom of God was brought into the open. Jesus came to destroy the devil's work (see 1 Jn. 3:8). This He did throughout His ministry as He healed the sick, cast out devils, and raised the dead. His final and total triumph over the powers of darkness in satan's kingdom was demonstrated in the Cross and resurrection. Jesus publicly displayed His triumph in the heavenlies by parading the conquered foes as His captives in the heavens (see Col. 2:15).

At Pentecost, Peter declared that the outpouring of the Holy Spirit was evidence that Christ has assumed the throne of David in the heavens (see Acts 2:32-36). Therefore, the rule of Christ is not in question. The King has a Kingdom, which is comprised of all those under the sphere of His rule. This is why the Church is an integral part of His Kingdom. But the Kingdom is larger than the Church, since He rules over much that is outside the Church and is ultimately destined to rule over all.

Nebuchadnezzar illustrates this concept. King Nebuchadnezzar became locked in madness until he was willing to acknowledge the extent of God's Kingdom rule (see Dan. 4:17,25,32). The King is on His throne, and from there, through the Spirit, He is establishing His rule—first over His people, then through His people in all the world. This is brought about as Christ sends us as the Father sent Him; empowers us with the same Spirit that He was empowered with; and works with us directly to establish His rule in the earth (see Jn. 17:18; Acts 1:8; 8:12). Meanwhile He stays at the Father's right hand in the heavens until His purpose is fully accomplished in our age. Then and then only will He return and submit the Kingdom of God to the Father once again (see Acts 3:21; 1 Cor. 15:15-25).

The Kingdom and the Church

The degree to which the Church readily submits itself to the rule of God determines the extent to which it moves in the power of the Kingdom and is able to demonstrate the authority of Christ's name in every situation of life. The Christian community is a Kingdom family. The establishing of His rule over our volatile emotions enables us to respond to the command of Jesus to "love one another" (see Jn. 13:34-35;

1 Jn. 3:11,14,16-18; 4:7-12,16-21). In Scripture, God places His emphasis on love as His rule in action, as opposed to personal feelings.

The primary operative principle in the Kingdom way of life is that of servanthood. We are seen as sons of the Kingdom when we serve one another as Christ taught and exampled (see Mt. 20:28; see also Mt. 3:11-15; Lk. 22:26-27). Conversely, the natural tendency of unregenerate man seeks to use everyone for personal ends and interests. In the Kingdom, the serving principle is at the heart of all ministry of elders to their people (see Lk. 22:24-27; Heb. 13:17; 1 Pet. 5:2). The foundation of Kingdom living and Kingdom ministry is that we are servants (see Gal. 5:13; 1 Pet. 4:10).

The Kingdom and Social Justice

The threshold of the throne of God from which God rules stands on the twin pillars of righteousness and justice (see Ps. 89:14; 97:2). Ours is not simply a message of blessing and a heart right with God, but of justice in every way for all men. The question of human justice cannot be pushed aside or relegated to the socio-economic or political spheres as something of no interest to the Christian community. Both righteousness and justice are basic to our gospel and our experience. Our understanding of what is right and our conviction of what is just come from a revelation of God's heart for mankind. God is not British or American. He is not a Westerner or an African. He is not a Baptist or a Pentecostal. Therefore, what is right does not spring from a bias in any national, denominational, cultural, or racial context. What is right and just is defined by God in the highest law of His Kingdom (see Lk. 10:27; Rom 13:9).

As children, which of us was not at some time or another frustrated with our being treated "unfairly" by others? Justice is when God demands all are treated alike—fairly. He condemns partiality or favoritism, since it is unfair and, therefore, unjust. There are times when God does not appear to be just, as the Psalmist said, "I have seen a wicked and ruthless man flourishing like a green tree in its native soil" (Ps. 37:35). However, God showed him that justice is for the long-term view (see Ps. 37:35-38; 73:17-20,27).

Isaiah highlighted our liberation mandate, saying,

Is not this the kind of fasting I have chosen: to loose the chains of injustice and untie the cords of the yoke, to set the oppressed free and break every yoke? Is it not to share your food with the hungry and to provide the poor wanderer with shelter—when you see the naked, to clothe him, and not to turn away from your own flesh and blood? (Isaiah 58:6-7)

Kingdom of God: The Invisible Presence

The retreat of evangelicals from the frontiers of social activism into personal soul saving has led to a tragic surrender of responsibility and contributed to the waning of evangelical influence and the devaluation of our gospel. For Christians to express their "concern" for the "dying souls of men" and take no responsibility for the pursuit of peace and justice or involve themselves in social concerns of our time is to live in conflict with God's purpose. The scope of God's restoration not only involves the redemption of souls, but also requires a return to our mandate to act on God's behalf in every situation in which we find ourselves. Redeemed man is to be on the cutting edge of the pursuit of justice, peace, environmental concerns, and social progress.

This does not mean that seeking to reach mankind with the gospel of reconciliation takes second place to social concerns. What it does mean is that we need to see man as an integrated whole, for the restoration process is a holistic one. The total redemption that God offers is for the total unredeemed person, affecting all aspects of human existence. God's restoration purpose not only gives us a concern for the soul of man in the gutter, but also provokes a response to seeing his external conditions changed.

We don't simply say to the homeless and hungry, "Get right with God"; rather, we seek to alleviate their suffering and look for a way to address the root causes of their situations. Jesus responded practically to the needs of the homeless, hungry, imprisoned, and dispossessed of His time, and in His life and preaching, He addressed the causes of those conditions. He probably would have gone down in history as one of the greatest philanthropists of all time had He not also preached! *The works of Jesus were received everywhere, but the words that preceded, accompanied, or followed those works struck as an axe to the root cause of human injustice.*

The engagement of the Christian community in humanitarian relief and development programs is desirable and laudable. However, our continued failure to address the causes that produce such needs is a shame to our time. Our *pastoral charge* on God's behalf is to love our fellow man, whereas our *prophetic calling* demands that we confront injustice wherever we find it. Prophetic restorers believe that it is not enough to stay in the comfort zone of good works; we must be prepared to continue our good works in the uncomfortable zone of prophetic confrontation. This points to the need for recognizing that apostles, prophets, evangelists, pastors, and teachers are set in the wider context of the Church in the world. We cannot afford to limit our function exclusively to religious settings and religious people.

To be baptized into Christ means that we are also baptized into the world's needs, into its deprivations, hurts, pains, injustices, and wrongs. We must give ourselves to actively working for change. The early

Kingdom of God: The Invisible Presence

Christian community turned the world upside down by its preaching, teaching, and practical living (see Acts 17:6 KJV). The practical living was not isolationist; it was outworked through the principles of the Kingdom of God in their everyday life.

The Kingdom and a Prophetic Voice

Before there can be personal or social transformation, there must, of necessity, be prophetic confrontation. When people do not have the fear of God, they lose the sense of the sanctity of life. In today's world—with the fear of God in little evidence—abortionists continue to seek to normalize the destruction of unborn children, while other so-called progressive "reformers" increase political and social pressure for euthanasia to become an accepted way of terminating life. Abortion is the consequence of cheapening the sanctity of life. It has become the ultimate form of birth control. Society has decided that terminating the life of an unborn child is acceptable in order to maintain the "convenience" of the parent(s). Similarly, advocates of euthanasia are asking the government and courts to step aside and allow people who are feeble and elderly to have their lives terminated "with dignity" for the convenience of the remaining family members. This is dangerously reminiscent of the Hitlerian view of life in Nazi Germany.

People may use sentimental and sympathetic arguments to support their actions, but none of these excuses or claimed reasons provide a justifiable basis for taking life. Suicide, abortion, homicide, and euthanasia are all assaults upon God's divine image and purpose in life. It is incomprehensible that the same society that can sanction the killing of untold millions of children in the womb every year should then be anguished and distraught over the widespread outbreaks of violence in society. When society shows collective violence on the unborn, it opens itself to violence on itself as it transfers its moral values to the next generation.

At the same time, let me say that where someone has participated in sanctioning abortion, had an abortion, or even performed an abortion, and has subsequently realized the wrong in this and repented, there is forgiveness with God. Restoration is not only the cleansing from sin and the extension of forgiveness, but also total recovery and reinstatement to fellowship with God. It is tragic when Christians catalog sins in such a way that some are forgivable, clearing the way for restoration of fellowship, while others somehow forever disqualify one from serving God in certain capacities. (These may vary according to the Christian denomination in which one is reared.) *Restoration has no cut-off point in forgiveness; rather, a full restoration to fellowship and servanthood is the divine purpose.*

Kingdom of God: The Invisible Presence

However bad our lives may have been, the grace and mercy of God is greater. Paul reminded the Corinthian believers of this, saying,

And that is what some of you were. But you were washed, you were sanctified, you were justified in the name of the Lord Jesus Christ and by the Spirit of our God (1 Corinthians 6:11).

The Kingdom and the Nations

Although the revelation of the Kingdom of God, which we receive through Christ and the apostles, is of a spiritual rule and government rather than a political or a material one, this does not mean that the political and material sphere of our world is unaffected by it. Although it does not redeem society, culture, politics, or the material world, it nevertheless does have a reforming influence upon world society.

As the Kingdom of God grows, so its influence enlarges. It is in this sense that Isaiah prophesied, "Of the increase of His government and peace there will be no end" (Is. 9:7). This is also the principle behind the vision in the Book of Daniel of the stone coming down, striking the image of the world empires, and growing to fill the whole earth (see Dan. 2:31-35,44-45; 7:13-14). Through this vision, God was foretelling the global success and purposes of God in His Kingdom.

The great commission given to the disciples to go and make disciples of all nations must not be read as a commission to save millions of individuals. Rather, in its context, the emphasis is on the corporate body of people that comprises a nation. So widespread will be the move of God's Spirit in these endtimes, so great will the harvest be, that the majority of the peoples in many nations will turn to Christ and seek to know from His servants the principles and precepts of the Kingdom as they are applied to the life of a society on earth. This will be our opportunity to disciple nations as Loraine Boettner stated in his book, *The Millennium*, "Evil in all its many forms eventually will be reduced to negligible proportions, that Christian principles will be the rule, not the exception, and that Christ will return to a truly Christianized world."[1]

The revelation of the New Testament clearly depicts that the vast majority of peoples in the earth will be born again at the conclusion of history. The fact that this is not apparently so at this time is irrelevant. The purpose of God does not progress by the ebb and flow of circumstances in history, but rather by the divine activity of God's Spirit working in conjunction with His Word.

---

1. Loraine Boettner, *The Millennium* (Philadelphia, Pennsylvania: Philadelphia Press, Presbytery & Reformed, 1958), 14.

Chapter 6

Triumphant Before the Cosmic Watchers

U PON HEARING OF GOD'S PURPOSE to ultimately bring everything under Christ's headship, people often challenge, "You don't expect that to happen *before* He comes, do you?" And when the restorer confidently asserts that he does, the usual rejoinder is, "Get real! Look around you," which is followed by a full recital of things the restorer already knows full well—that the world is filled with violence, corruption, dishonesty, and greed, with much of it structurally undergirded by governments and political powers that are allied with demonic spirits.

This apparent conflict presents the following challenge: Do you believe the Word of God or the voices that highlight visible circumstances? The Lordship of Christ must be asserted over *all* things, *including our thinking.* Our natural tendency to unbelief and negative thinking must be brought into submission to His Lordship. Restorers must remain radically committed to the triumph of His rule over all things—both internal and external to ourselves.

Two thousand years ago Jesus demonstrated His Lordship in every sphere, including these:

- *Over nature* by walking on the water and stilling the storm (see Mt. 14:22-33; Mk. 6:45-51; Jn. 6:16-21);

- *Over demonic spirits* by liberating many such as the man of Gadara (see Mt. 8:28-34; Mk. 5:1-17; Lk. 8:26-37);

- *Over sickness* by healing multitudes (see Mt. 12:15);

- *Over the composition of the elements* that make up physical matter by changing water into wine (see Jn. 2:1-11);

- *Over the devious hearts of men* by refuting the accusations and questions of Pharisees and leaving them tongue-tied (see Mt. 22:41-46; Mk. 12:35-37; Lk. 20:27-40; Jn. 8:3-11);

- *And ultimately over death itself* by His raising of the widow's son and by His own resurrection (see Lk. 7:11-15; Col. 2:15).

Triumphant Before the Cosmic Watchers

The greatest question in the end of time will be, who rules? God's ultimate purpose is to establish Christ's Lordship over the total cosmos through the Church (see Col. 1:18).

A Cosmic View

To truly grasp the scope of God's work in achieving this requires a cosmic perspective. Paul unfolds the mystery of Christ in such a way that our thinking must expand well beyond individual redemption, even go beyond the redeemed community (see Col. 1:15-22). God wants us to see the incredible length, breadth, depth, and height of the working of His Spirit in securing the inheritance for Christ the Son, in whom, through whom, and for whom it all exists (see Rom. 11:36; Eph. 3:17-20). Everything that has been created to serve the purpose of God as part of God's inheritance for the Son will be restored. That is, it will be brought back from evil domination and from serving evil ends, enacting unjust laws, and supporting unfair practices in its oppression of mankind. Everything will be restored to serving God's original creation purpose of expressing His love for man, looking after man's welfare, and serving righteous ends and justice for all in society.

At the heart of God's cosmic plan is the Church. Paul presented us with a revelation of our place and purpose before the cosmic watchers of the visible and invisible worlds in his letter to the Ephesians:

*His intent was that **now, through the church,** the manifold wisdom of God should be made known to the rulers and authorities in the heavenly realms* (Ephesians 3:10).

The unveiling of this mystery implies that invisible angelic beings are being taught by what they see of the effect of the working of His Spirit in and through the Church. They stand enthralled by the ways and wisdom of God at work in and through the Church to advance the cosmic restoration of all things to Christ.

But none of this can succeed without overcoming challenges from the enemy. The cosmic struggle evident throughout the life and ministry of Christ continues in our present day as the risen Lord strides forth in His earthly Body—the Church—and strikes the forces of darkness with the two-edged sword of truth. The end of this conflict will see the deliverance of the nations from destructive powers and their readiness to learn the ways of God (see Is. 2:3). Throughout the new age and ages to come the ever-increasing rule of God over all things will continue to move everything forward to a fullness as yet unimagined (see Is. 9:6-7).

The universe does not come to its fullness with the return of Christ. It is freed from restraints on its development with the liberation of the "sons of God" into their fullness. It is from this point that all things in Heaven and earth move forward in a fullness only known as yet in the sovereign mind of God.

The Triumph in the Cross

The empty cross and tomb straddle the boundary line between this age and the one to come, where Christ the pioneer/trailblazer has already gone. Every time we triumph in any circumstance or situation opposed to us—every time we heal the sick, cast out devils, lead people to faith in Christ, receive answers to our prayers, experience the divine presence, fellowship among His people, and share His life in the everyday world of our existence—we are tasting of the powers of the age to come (see Heb. 6:5). This is the context in which Paul introduces the Church to the necessity of its engagement in spiritual warfare (see Eph. 6:12). He envisions the Church in powerful assault upon the kingdom of darkness.

At the Cross, religion stood naked in its rejection of the Son of God. Rome, the greatest political power of the day, stood condemned for its complicity in the death of Christ. Increasingly troubled by the controversial and radical prophet whose words and works transcended the physical realm in which their political structures were rooted, the religious and political leaders agreed: Jesus had to be silenced—He had to be killed. Walter Wink says, "...the just man is killed. The embodiment of God's will is executed by God's servants. The incarnation of the orderly principles of the universe is crucified by the guardians of order. The very nucleus of spiritual power in the universe is destroyed by the spiritual powers."[1] Both the religious and the political worlds were revealed for what they had become in reality: wicked, ugly, alien, and opposed to God. This is why allegiance to Christ must supersede religion and politics, whatever the consequence, at every point in history. The martyrdom suffered by members of the early Church in Rome's arenas was a powerful demonstration of overriding allegiance to the Lordship of Christ. In more recent times, the hundreds of thousands of Christians who have suffered and continue to suffer for their faith in prisons around the world serve as poignant reminders that the cosmic battle of visibly establishing the Lordship of Christ over all else is far from over.

To understand the triumph of Christ in the Cross throughout the cosmos, it is important we understand the peoples' worldview at the time of Christ. The people had no demarcation line in their minds between spirits and systems or between demons and despots. In their thinking, the visible and invisible worlds interlocked in their thinking and flowed easily

---

1. Walter Wink, *Naming the Powers* (Philadelphia, Pennsylvania: Fortress Press, 1984), 114.

from one to the other. This fluidity of thought allowed Jesus, Paul, and others to speak of authorities, powers, rulers, principalities, thrones, and dominions without the need to define these terms. As part of the prevailing worldview, the meanings of these terms were understood from the context of the dialogue in which they were used.

Modern theologians and scholars invest considerable time defining each biblical term and considering etymologies and the various root combinations used by the biblical authors—all in the hope of understanding what is written and what its significance is. But the overlap in usage of various terms, combined with the observation that some words are used interchangeably, leads us to the conclusion that a better understanding will be gained if we view these studied passages as an integrated whole. For example, when the Scripture speaks of "principalities and powers," "all rule and authority," or "every ruler, and every authority and power," the apostle is speaking of powers that are visible *and* invisible, heavenly *and* earthly, spiritual *and* human, demonic *and* political, ethereal *and* structural (see Rom 8:38-39; Eph. 1:21; Eph. 3:10 KJV; Col. 2:10 NAS; 1 Cor. 15:24 NRS).

Today, the worldview of the western mind has largely discounted the spirit world, for it has locked itself into a materialistic perspective. The nearest that many people get to acknowledging forces beyond the material is when they psychoanalyze individuals in whom there appears to be abnormality or breakdown and recommend psychiatric help or therapy. Their whole approach, however, views individuals as victims of the pressures of society or the material world in which they live, and their diagnosis and treatment ignore any possible spiritual dimension to their problems.

On the other hand, many Charismatic Christians completely ignore the powerful influence of modern social structures and the oppression that the socio-political world exerts upon individuals. They see all recurrent problems as the result of unseen spirits at work. This has led to widespread abuse in Charismatic circles, as people already needing help are further disturbed by being subjected to forms of biblically unfounded exorcism that amounts to nothing more than physical and mental abuse. Today God is restoring clear understanding on "deliverance" ministry that is both valid and biblical. *Restorers* assert that, wherever we are called upon to liberate men and women from their oppressions and bondage, we must do so while recognizing the need to deal with the root of the problem in the visible *and* invisible worlds. The authority of Christ must be established over *both*. Failure to give adequate attention to both areas will leave the person vulnerable to further oppression, and he or she will likely continue to be a victim of a one-dimensional deliverance ministry.

Triumphant Before the Cosmic Watchers

The Cross, master-minded by satan in unholy conspiracy with the religious and political leaders of that day, actually proved to be a catastrophic disaster for the enemy. The demonic spirits were totally routed, and Christ triumphantly paraded them as a spectacle across the heavens (see Col. 2:15). In doing this, He displayed God's power as the greatest in the universe. In the resurrection and ascension, God established His Son as cosmic Lord, seating Him at His own right hand.

Living With the Paradox

Having said this, we still cannot escape the fact that we live in the dynamic tension of the *already* and the *not yet.* Christ *has* triumphed and *is yet* to triumph; He is already the mighty conqueror who has rendered the enemy completely powerless, and yet death is still seen as the last enemy to be overcome (see 1 Cor. 15:26; Heb. 2:14-15). We are located in the *already happened and yet to happen* paradox. It is a *completed* work and yet a work *to be completed.* In the interim period between the already accomplished triumph of Christ and the grand finale of its ultimate manifestation in His return, we find ourselves engaged in cosmic warfare. The nearer we get to the truth, the nearer we get to God's reality, the more the dividing line between natural and supernatural, visible and invisible, and time and eternity begins to disappear. As the writer to Hebrews says,

> ...*In putting everything under him, God left nothing that is not subject to him. Yet at present we do not see everything subject to him. But we see Jesus, who was made a little lower than the angels, now crowned with glory and honor because He suffered death, so that by the grace of God He might taste death for everyone* (Hebrews 2:8-9).

In other words, despite our paradoxical experience, our hope lies in Christ—who is affirmed by the Father in the ascension and glorification at His right hand. He is the first of many sons to glory, and because He is there, we shall also be: "In bringing many sons to glory, it was fitting that God, for whom and through whom everything exists, should make the author of their salvation perfect through suffering" (Heb. 2:10).

One of the Church's greatest songs of triumph is the doxology in Romans 8:31-39, which hinges on the theme, "If God is for us, who can be against us?" The rest of the song seems to rise as an anthem of praise from millions of voices saying, "No one, nothing, nothing at all—nothing in Heaven, earth, or under the earth, nothing in our present experience, nothing in our future experience, nothing acting from within itself against us, nothing acting on behalf of others against us, no system, no threat, no intimidation, no law, no unjust judgment, no mass revolt, no peer pressure, no structural violence, no demon, no political or economic system, no socio-political pressure, nothing in the invisible or visible worlds either in our existing space galaxy or in unseen galaxies, in this age or the age to come—can separate us from the love of God that is in Christ Jesus our Lord. The cosmic Christ is cosmic Lord, and He is for us. This being true, who can, indeed, who would dare, be against us?!" In this passage, Paul seems intent on making as broad a sweep of the spatial-temporal, terrestrial, and extraterrestrial spheres as possible, to convince the Church of its present triumph in Christ: *Christ must reign until He has put all His enemies under His feet* (see 1 Cor. 15:24-25).

Paul preached what is now actual in Christ's resurrection: He has completely defeated all powers and rendered impotent their ability to unrestrainedly and unquestionably exert dominion over God's people, and this will, at some future time, be cosmically demonstrated as the eternal state for all things. This is when He will put down the last enemy—death—and bring everything beneath His feet. Christ has already established His rule over the powers of darkness, and in His second coming, He will subject them totally to Himself before submitting everything to God that He might be all in all (see 1 Cor. 15:27-28).

By faith, we can bring that ultimate victory into every situation on a daily basis. Tomorrow becomes today as we learn to walk in the steps of Him who has already triumphed.

Understanding God's plan of restoration means that we don't indulge in a shallow and unhealthy preoccupation with Heaven, which has isolated the Church from the experience of ordinary people for far too long. The Church now finds it difficult to persuade society that it has a message that is relevant because its focus has been almost exclusively on the hereafter. To the uninitiated, the Christian message has all too often been, "Heaven by and by—sweet pie in the sky." This is not the gospel of the Kingdom. *The message of the rule of God in righteousness and justice is a radical one that cuts to the core of human existence.* I am not saying there is no Heaven. I firmly believe that redeemed humanity will ultimately enjoy the Heaven of God's presence as much as the earth filled with His presence. But ours is not an escapist message; it is a redemptive message. Our triumphant testimony is that Christ has conquered the powers of darkness and that we—in Christ—can rule in life now (see Rom. 5:17).

Chapter 7

Where His Presence Is Pleased to Dwell

PEOPLE WERE CONVERTED and baptized into the early Church with the conviction that they and their whole household would be saved (see Acts 16:31; 18:8). These Christian families were the primary centers of God's life and faith among men and frequently formed the nucleus of what could be called "church in the home" (see Rom. 16:5; 1 Cor. 16:19; Philem. 2).

Throughout the last two millenniums the Church has evolved from its simple beginnings of extended families gathered in the home to its current state of highly complex systems and networks of Christian congregations around the world, many of which can only be described as "mega-churches." In Latin America and Africa, some of these churches are in excess of 70,000 members, and increasingly in the USA, many churches now number between 10,000 and 20,000, with a congregation in Seoul, Korea, reaching as many as half a million. The trend has moved away from the small neighborhood church to large church congregations, which are often conveniently located on major highways or thoroughfares.

Proponents of this trend cite the following benefits:

- The larger size of these congregations creates greater impact and influence throughout the community.

- One is able to draw together a highly trained professional staff that can "run the church," handle the meetings, deal with the tax authorities and banks, etc., which is not always the case with smaller churches.

- Burgeoning finances provide these groups with the ability to do so much more in the work of missions around the world.

- The mega-sized cities of our generation—with many now numbering from 10 to 20 million (and some even larger)—require large-scale testimony.

- They can underwrite the huge costs of modern communications such as TV programing.

Restorers also believe that God intends dynamic churches with sufficient numbers, ability, gift, and finances to meet the challenges of the deepening darkness of the endtimes. However, restorers also assert that we must face the fact that, generally, no more than 15 percent of a church of 100, and as low as 10 percent in a church of 1,000, are *actively* engaged in the ministry and meetings on a regular basis. That means that somewhere between 85 percent and 90 percent of the people in most churches are merely congregational attendees!

This highlights the paradigm shift between the first century Church and that of the twentieth century. The early Church was comprised of a highly mobile, highly motivated, *outward-bound* people on a mission to reach the ends of the earth. The Church of the twentieth century has increasingly become a static, *building-bound* congregation sharing a few hours of common time each week and being serviced by a small core of people who "run" the meetings and church programs.

Although the earliest Christian meetings were initially inside the temple and its courtyards, more intimate gatherings of the Church quickly spread into private homes (see Acts 2:46; 12:12). The home proved to be the most advantageous place to meet, especially in the cities of the Diaspora. At Corinth, Aquila and Priscilla had the church in their home; later, Paul fellowshipped and ministered in the home of Titius Justus, next door to the Jewish synagogue (see Acts 18:7). The larger homes of wealthier individuals often became the place where a number of smaller family home groups would gather together to share fellowship (see Rom. 16:23; 1 Cor. 14:23).

For the early Church, there were definite advantages to meeting in a home:

- *The privacy of the setting*, especially where meeting as Christians was against the law.

- *Christians could pursue their exercise of the charismata* (gifts of the Spirit) and break bread without being misunderstood or judged by the uninitiated public.

- *The costs* of such meetings were minimal.

- *It was easy to network* the community of believers across the city and region, which made it so much more conducive for fellowship and friendship throughout the day.

- *Intimacy and friendship were cultivated*, and as a consequence, each member of the church felt secure to participate in the gatherings.

- *Each Christian could develop* in their contribution of gift in the meeting.

From the beginning, the early Church was surrounded by a hostile religious and political world that was incensed by the fact that the controversial troublemaker Jesus could not be disposed of. His resurrection was proclaimed everywhere, and the absence of a body to confirm His death—together with hundreds of witnesses to His living presence—left both Jewish religious leaders and Roman officials in great difficulty.

Despite the open hostility, the early Christians (once they were empowered by God's Holy Spirit) gave themselves zealously to the proclamation of the good news of God's love, power, salvation, and Kingdom. Since the world around them was not neutral, it was impossible for anyone joining them to be neutral toward the world (see Jn. 15:18-20). To embrace Christ and become part of His extended family was to take up a cross daily to follow Him (see Mt. 16:24). The fact that the churches in the home were illicit communities and that it was a capital offense to be a Christian did not stop God's people from multiplying and growing across the nations as the family of God.

At the helm of this advance were the apostles and prophets. Apostolic teams emerged with a breadth and diversity of gift strengths. They ensured that networking churches were established on the firm foundation of Christ. This meant not simply teaching doctrine, but also daily living (walking) in the life they had found in Christ. The apostles knew that *no foundation is truly laid in a Christian community until it becomes the authentic, practiced lifestyle of the members of that community.*

In today's world of six billion people, the majority will soon be in mega-cities. There is a place for the large mega-church witness, but these churches should integrate hundreds, if not thousands, of expressions of God's Church in homes. The two expressions should not be in competition; they both have their place in revealing "the manifold wisdom of God" (Eph. 3:10).

Streets to Live In

The natural tendency of the human mind is to imprison itself inside thought tramlines. We must not confine God's purpose to being outworked in mega-church or house-church situations. Look at Isaiah's prophecy of God's intention to restore "paths" or "streets" to live in. Western society, in its inordinate desire for privatism, seeks to live in the detached houses of present times rather than in the close community life experienced by previous generations.

My childhood and upbringing were in a terrace house (town house) in a street with 42 houses on one side and 40 on the other. In this context with the close proximity of life you discovered a largeness to your family beyond the few who lived in your actual house; the extended family included deep relationships with many others in the street. There was a mutual concern and regard for the welfare of each other. Each family was its neighbor's keeper. Life tended to be one of shared experience, even to the passing on of packages of clothes from one family to another as they were outgrown by the children. Excitement and happenings in one home would be shared with the street; often in celebration there were street parties much as today in some areas where they have street carnivals. Equally, when grief came to a home, it could not come to one alone, but it came to the many. Children who were aspiring for better things through education were not simply encouraged by their father and mother, but also by many other uncles, aunts, and friends in the street. In time of need no one was alone; the street in which you lived was a living community of which you were continually a part.

Isaiah's prophecy of the endtimes is that the Church in all its growth will rediscover this same sense of intimacy of life together. In this sense what Jesus spoke of as being *His experience* of nakedness, hunger, the aloneness of prisons, etc. (see Mt. 25:31-46), was the consequence of the way the least of His people was treated, and His declarations support Isaiah's prophecy of the community of God.

The prophet foresaw a time when God would "restore" the community life of His people. Privacy would yield to intimacy; separation would give way to integration. God's people would have not castles to live in, but streets. Gone will be the days of isolationist religion, of two hours of religious interaction per week. The community of God will be seen to be a joyful life of community.

Chapter 8

No Longer Alone

*"Forgive us that with the Cross as starting point
we have made the Christian
faith a bland and easy going way of life."*[1]

Christianity today is all too often portrayed as a very self-centered religion. We have become preoccupied with "my health, my finances, my job, my family." Our prayers tend to be locked into these circles. There is an urgent need for the restoration of the sense of community. Our interdependence on each other ought not be a "safety

---

1. Ernest T. Campbell, *Where Cross the Crowded Ways: Prayers for a City Pastor* (New York: Associated Press, 1973). Born in 1915, Ernest Campbell was a former minister of Riverside Church, New York City.

net" should my needs fail to be met, but a divinely ordained context of positive living.

This bonding of the early Christian communities was the result of something stronger than a set of common beliefs; they were *joined by covenant* together. The biblical concept and reality of covenant defies dictionary definition. Words are too small to convey what is contained in the biblical concept of covenant. For example, Webster's Dictionary defines covenant as "a formal, solemn, and binding agreement."[2] This is a very clear, but totally inadequate, definition.

Covenant goes deeper than the definition suggests, and it is certainly wider in its implications than people first realize. Covenant extends beyond Scripture and Christianity. It permeates the whole of life. It is the bonding power in marriage, business transactions, holiday agreements, insurance policies, government and personal pensions, club memberships, international defense agreements, peace agreements, trading agreements, extradition treaties between countries, citizenship, residency agreements—the list is virtually endless. The truth is that covenant is *pervasive to the whole of life*, and its understanding and practice affect all people, whether they are aware

---

2. *Webster's Ninth New Collegiate Dictionary* (Springfield, Massachusetts: Merriam-Webster, Inc., 1986).

of it or not. This is why its violation and the consequences that follow its violation are far more wide-reaching than commonly realized. Millions of people are experiencing the painful consequences of broken covenant without even knowing that this is the root cause of what is happening to them.

Individualism had no place in the thinking of the covenant society of Israel. Indeed, to the Hebrew the greatest curse of all to befall man is find himself alone. The prophet Jeremiah called out in anguish, complaining, "I sat alone because of Your hand, for You have filled me with indignation" (Jer. 15:17b NKJ). The Psalmist described the pain and torment of being alone when he said, "I watch, and am as a sparrow alone upon the house top. Mine enemies reproach me all the day..." (Ps. 102:7-8 KJV). Hosea described the misery and torture of Israel by calling them "a wild ass alone by himself" (Hos. 8:9 KJV).

The people of God are not a collection of individuals, but are a community of people joined and integrated in Christ as one new man. The new covenant does for the people of God, the Church, what the old covenant did for Israel, only more so. The covenant caused them to enjoy peaceful relations together. *Shalom* was their word not simply of greeting, but expressed their whole life as a people.

Shalom or *peace* signifies the state of relations inside the covenant community. Ezekiel and Isaiah referred to the covenant of peace (see Ezek. 34:25; 37:26; Is. 54:10). Peace was that relationship enjoyed together in the love of God. It described their day-to-day experience of the covenant community. As one Danish theologian put it: "If everything that comes under the term of covenant were dissolved, existence would fall to pieces, because no soul can live an isolated life....therefore the annihilation of the covenant would not only be the ruin of society but the dissolution of each individual soul."[3]

Unfortunately, those who lack understanding concerning covenant and its violation are often the ones who most need to grasp its significance; that is, those who have entered the New Covenant in Christ. Covenant affects our relationships with all that surrounds us, and it determines the *quality* of our fellowship with God, family, other believers, and society. Any breach of covenant can have the following effects in our relationships:

- *With God*—The heavens will become as brass to us (see Deut. 28:23 KJV). God said that if we regard iniquity in our heart, the *Lord will not hear us* (see Ps. 66:18 KJV).

- *With our family*—Our prayers will be hindered; where we do not walk in upright relationship

3. J. Pedersen, *Israel: Its Life and Culture* (London: Oxford University Press, 1926), 308.

within the covenant of marriage, we leave ourselves open to this and other ills (see 1 Pet. 3:7).

- *With the Church*—The hypocrisy of claiming to be
  one Body while remaining divided from each
  other violates the reality of the New Covenant
  and opens us to all kinds of sickness, even pre-
  mature death (see 1 Cor. 11:30).

- *With society*—We violate our purpose in this
  world. This world is affected for the good when
  confronted by our integrity and good works. We
  are meant to communicate Christ to the wider
  society around us through our good works (see
  1 Pet. 2:12).

- *With the environment*—We become destroyers
  rather than guardians of the earth. Adam was
  created to protect and serve his environment;
  instead, he chose to pursue his self-interest at
  the expense of all else. In pursuing that same
  self-interest, his progeny continue to poison the
  earth's atmosphere as well as its land and seas.
  As a result, the world's population is now subjected to a wide range of respiratory ailments,
  sicknesses, skin disorders, cancers, and an esca-
  lating development of new horrific diseases...
  (see Rom. 8:19-21).

God has never dealt with man on any basis other
than covenant, from Adam right up to the present
time. Various specific covenants are described in

Scripture, each of them revealing more of God's nature and purpose for man. Outside of Christ, we were strangers to these "covenants of promise," but now we are participants in these same covenants through our relationship with Him (see Eph. 2:12-13 KJV). The various biblical covenants should not be understood as dispensational; that is, each lasting a fixed period, only to be cast aside at the advent of a new one. The revelation of God is continuous, and the continuing revelation of His person and purpose for man is accompanied by a calling to a new depth of covenant commitment. Biblical covenants prior to Jesus *were "swallowed" into the New Covenant, like a river reaching the sea. All the covenants prior to Christ were focused toward Him, and in Him—the New Covenant—they all find their fulfillment.*

The early Christians never considered life outside covenant. The commitment to Christ, to one another, and to God's ultimate purpose for all things was rooted in their radical commitment to live covenantally, and it generated a readiness to be radical in it, no matter what the cost. Whatever their circumstances or condition, they knew it was tied to their keeping or breaking of covenant.

Restoration of our understanding of this challenges us to new levels of commitment, and it causes us to progress to higher levels of living, all the way to the fullness of Christ described by Paul in his letter to the Ephesians (see Eph. 3:13-21).

Lateral Covenant

Jesus taught covenant to the disciples in a variety of ways, and it was most strongly communicated by His own example. His utter giving of Himself to the Father's will, their welfare, and the people's needs—almost without consideration of His own—challenged them. He signified the depth of covenant when He spoke of their "abiding" in Him (see Jn. 15:4-10 KJV). This phrase expresses the union between Christ and His Church, which is meant to be inseparable in life. The phrase, *abide in Me*, means to have no consciousness of unrighteousness separating you from Christ in your fellowship with Him. It also implies that you are not engaged in any activity that He cannot be a part of. On the positive side, "abiding" is descriptive of our union with Him in life in all its activities and of our dependence on Him in every matter that requires wisdom, decision, direction, or action. It is being careful in our commitment and at all times maintaining uninhibited fellowship with Christ and His people.

Therefore, in coming into Christ you come into covenant with all others in Christ. You do not choose the members of this covenant. Our relationship together is not on a "pick and choose" basis, for to be in relationship with Christ is to be in relationship with the whole family of God in Christ. However, a new question now arises: How do we *experientially* live out the covenant together with others in Christ? It is at this point that restorers are sometimes accused of seeking to introduce a "different" covenant basis for relationship between Christians, one that is "outside" the New Covenant in Christ. This is blatantly untrue. What we *do* seek is to "*practicalize*" the New Covenant; we are anxious to make the New Covenant *experiential* for all believers.

Achieving God's purpose requires the commitment of all parties to a *proactive* covenant relationship. All other purposes, relationships, or pursuits in life are subservient to the keeping of the New Covenant. Yet this does not preclude the existence of horizontal covenants *within* the New Covenant. In fact, as pointed out at the beginning of this chapter, horizontal covenants are made every day, and they are not the exclusive domain of Christians. Those people afraid of horizontal covenants within the New Covenant community do either of the following:

1. *They don't understand God's covenant nature, or*

2. *They are not prepared for the commitment that covenant keeping demands.*

No Longer Alone

Some Christians, looking for an excuse to escape covenant issues, choose to ignore covenant teaching. They feel that if they remain ignorant of covenants, then they cannot suffer for violating covenant. This is wrong thinking. It is like a man who, knowing that he is not in right fellowship with his brother, thinks that as long as he doesn't take the Eucharist (communion) with him, he will not be judged. It is like the adulterer who believes that as long as his wife doesn't know about his illicit affair, no one is hurt. Avoiding the issues of covenant life leads to self-delusion and, ultimately, self-destruction.

Today, everybody wants to assert their rights, be they women's rights, minority rights, children's rights, human rights, employment rights, or democratic rights. All that may be fine, but how about we also take up our *responsibilities*? The obligations of living in covenant with others are part of God's grand design for transforming us into the likeness of Jesus. One cannot opt out of God's design without experiencing the consequences. There is no possible way of keeping covenant vertically without doing the same horizontally, which is why God provides the means for us to experience covenant on a very practical basis. This God-designed experience includes commitment and accountability to a specific group of people—the local church body.

Maintaining Covenant

Our *relationship* in Christ through regeneration is settled and forever intact; it can never be broken. Nevertheless Jesus' statement, "*If you abide in Me*" (see Jn. 15:4-8 KJV), indicates that our *fellowship* in Christ is subject to constant assault and may be broken at times. The emphasis throughout the New Testament on restoring broken fellowship with other members of the Body of Christ is a reminder that even though we cannot "change our relatives" inside the family of God, we can damage our fellowship within the family.

The Bible says that one hallmark of the endtimes is that men will be "covenantbreakers" (Rom. 1:31 KJV). This is in the general society, not the Christian community alone. God is concerned as to how society handles covenant just as He is about the rest of their lifestyle, whether righteous or unrighteous. Great issues are at stake here. Nowhere is this covenant issue at a higher level than in the experience of the people of God.

The highest expression of our commitment to each other in the New Covenant is found at the communion table, which is why God is so clear about ridding ourselves of all hypocrisy before we practice this sacrament. To share in the Eucharist while separated in heart from each other opens up the dreadful prospect of bringing judgment upon ourselves. Paul says that for this reason "many among you are weak and sick, and a number of you have fallen asleep [died]" (1 Cor. 11:30), showing how important it is to be in right fellowship in the covenant of the family of God. *You can anoint someone with oil repeatedly with fervent prayer for their healing, but if their sickness is a consequence of wrong attitudes or broken fellowship within the family of God, no healing will come until fellowship is restored and the damaged relationship made whole.* The apostle Peter said that judgment begins in the house of God (see 1 Pet. 4:17).

Covenant Discipline

Unfortunately, the Church as the covenant community has become compromised throughout the centuries by its unwillingness to deal with wrong and wrongdoers in the covenant community. Under the pretense of "loving" and "not being judgmental," we have opened the door to all kinds of evil in the covenant community. The world is not shocked to hear of moral scandals, financial impropriety, and even child abuse in churches. Frequently churches accept people who are under discipline in some other church and, in effect, short circuit God's purpose in discipline. Churches are failing to challenge ongoing sin (see 1 Thess. 5:14; 1 Tim. 5:20), and they sometimes serve as "hideouts" for those on the run from themselves. However, before looking at judgment in dealing with offenses, let us first look at judgment as a positive affirmation of life.

The very first example of judgment was God standing back, looking at each act of His creation, and pronouncing it "good." This was judgment in a positive way; it was assessing with a view to being satisfied. Sometimes, as in the creation of man, judgment is with a view to *adjustment.* When He looked at the solitary Adam, God said, "It is *not good* for the man to be alone" (Gen. 2:18a). *There was no flaw in God's creation of man, but there was a lack of fullness* in that Adam had no corresponding human relationship with whom to fellowship or with whom he could fulfill God's intention of filling the earth with God's image and likeness. When God completed man in making woman, He enabled man to be fulfilled in Himself and to fulfill God's purpose in the earth.

Throughout the history of God's covenant people, Israel, God's judgment was in continuous action. Wherever God was pleased with Israel, blessing flowed abundantly. Wherever God was displeased, curses came. (See Deuteronomy 28.) Both experiences were the consequence of judgment. *The purpose of judgment was to keep the people of God pure, productive, and progressing toward fullness.*

Likewise today, we need to recover the place and practice of righteous judgment in the Church. People often say, "You should not judge." This is contrary to what God has commanded us to do; we are told to "test everything" and to "make a right judgment" (Jn. 7:24; 1 Thess. 5:21). Jesus' parable about trying to remove a mote from your brother's eye when you have a beam in your own was *to emphasize where judgment should begin*, not to teach that there should be *no* judgment. We must first judge ourselves and, where necessary, repent and adjust, for it is only then that we can help others (see Mt. 7:5 KJV).

People's lack of commitment to building according to the Word of God has produced a confusing mixture in terms of what is permitted or tolerated in the lifestyle of the covenant community. The apostle Paul was clear and firm in resisting the intrusion of *external heresy* and in purging and purifying the Church of *internal corruption*. The immorality that arose in the Corinthian church (where a man was having sexual relations with his stepmother) was inexplicably tolerated. An incensed Paul addressed the church apostolically and brought godly judgment. It is interesting to note the end result that the apostle was seeking to achieve; that is, that we might *be what we really are* (see 1 Cor. 5:7). What we really are is a righteous people before God. Permitting wrongdoing to remain unjudged is to sin against both our nature and our calling in Christ. God's intention in discipline is to restore us *experientially* to our proper state and standing, and even in this extreme case at Corinth, the goal of the judgment was to restore the offender. Failure to judge wrongdoing in a covenant community sends out the wrong message. We must be wise, firm, and compassionate in any judgment and discipline process, maintaining the focus of its purpose. Judgment is not for *destruction*; it is for *restoration*.

Someone once remarked sadly that the Christian army is the only army that shoots its wounded. There are many thousands of Christians who have made bad mistakes, fallen into sin, and damaged themselves and others. In coming to repentance, these same people have found mercy, forgiveness, and grace with God, *but rejection from His people.* Today thousands of quality people have no effective place of ministry within the Church because the Church has refused to restore them, even though God has forgiven them. To the people who feel rejected, I say, "Wake up! Don't sit at home sucking your thumb holding a private pity party. If the covenant community lacks the grace to make room for your input, give yourself as Christ did and be the servant of all people. Be a faithful servant of God, and pursue a place of influence in the wider world around you, where you can compassionately bring Christ to those in need. Be strong and work for social and legislative change, human justice, and a better society, and do it knowing this: You are not serving in some inferior capacity in God's eyes; you will one day hear Him say, 'Well done, good and faithful servant' " (Mt. 25:23).

Some say that God forgets when He forgives. This is not strictly accurate, since forgetting is a human weakness. The Bible says God chooses to "remember no more" (Heb. 10:17; see also Jer. 31:34). This is very different from forgetting. God is saying that *He accepts our repentance and has determined not to recall our fault in any further fellowship with us.* It is dealt with. Neither will He determine our future by our past mistakes now that they are forgiven, for that would require that He remember our wrongs.

Our approach to discipline within the covenant community must be Christlike. We are not to be weak and afraid to deal with sin, but neither must we be cruel in our discipline and crush the penitent. We must be firm in our call for repentance, yet we must also be as generous in our mercy as God is to forgive the penitent. Although restoration to fellowship does not necessarily or automatically mean reinstatement to the same place or role in ministry, it does mean that we will look for every possible way to encourage and help the repentant person to rediscover a meaningful place of service whereby he or she can please God and be fulfilled him or herself, a place where we can all benefit again from his or her grace gift among us (see Gal. 6:1).

Covenant Continuity

God's covenants in every generation were all made as covenants of continuity with a line of faith. This line of faith provided God with His entry in each generation. God never allowed the spiritual state of His people to deteriorate to the point where everything of the line of faith that had gone ahead—their testimony and commitment to His purpose—was lost. God always spoke to and through a heart of faith that acted as the bridge to the incoming generation. His covenant, therefore, was perpetual. One example of this was the prophet Samuel, who served in the closing years of Eli in preparation to lead a new generation. Each generation must serve God's purpose in the freshness of its own word and vision from God, but the hallmark of any generation's authenticity of faith in God's purpose is that their witness and testimony is a continuation of what has gone before through the thin line of faith. There's a continuity of covenant in the generations.

Chapter 9

The Restoration of Apostles and Prophets

SO MUCH THAT was clearly understood and practiced in the early Church has been lost or become obscured with the passage of time. This is particularly true with regard to understanding the nature and function of the ascension gifts of Christ in His Church (see Eph. 4:11-16). In this final chapter, I wish to focus on two of the gifts mentioned because they are the *key ministries* to be restored at this historic juncture in God's plan of restoration. They are the *apostles* and *prophets*.

In place of apostles and prophets have come archbishops, cardinals, bishops, and executive boards. The claim that Christ is restoring apostles and prophets in His Church today meets with everything from surprise to resistance from the religious establishment.

A pastor once challenged me by asking, "Why do we need to be concerned with apostles and prophets today? We have got on very well without them so far!" It might be true to say that the Church has "got on" without these ministries, *but can it really be said we have got on "well" without them?*

- Would we say it is "well" when the one Church of Jesus Christ has now got an estimated 250,000 denominations and sects dividing it?

- Would we say "well" when—to a large extent—the Church's testimony is weak, and its voice has become increasingly irrelevant?

- Would we say "well" when the power of the resurrected life of Christ in the supernatural is rarely seen?

- Would we say "well" when the Church, ravaged by dissent, continues to compromise itself on some of the most fundamental moral issues of our time rather than giving clear prophetic leadership?

Paul declared that none of the "gifts" of the ascended Lord, including apostles and prophets, would pass away "until" the Church reaches *unity of the faith and full measure of the fullness of Christ* (see Eph. 4:13). Who would dare claim that this has been achieved? The word *until* is the key to understanding *the present necessity for* and the *continuing restoration of* apostles and prophets in the Church. It is illogical to claim that we need the evangelists, pastors, and teachers, but not the apostles and prophets, when God has distinctly given them for the purpose of attaining fullness in the Church.

In order to avoid unnecessary misunderstanding, let me clearly say that *we are not claiming* that present-day apostles are the same as the original twelve. In fact, the Scriptures show us *three* categories of apostles:

1. *The unique apostleship* of the Lord Jesus Christ Himself (see Heb. 3:1).

2. *The twelve that Jesus chose to be His apostles*, with Matthias replacing Judas following the resurrection of Christ (see Acts 1:21-22). These twelve are unique as the foundation stones of the new order. They are the "apostles of the Lamb" (Rev. 21:14).

3. *The post-ascension apostles* who are gifts of the ascended Christ (see Eph. 4:7-11).[1] Paul was

---

1. There are those who argue that Matthias was not one of the twelve, but that God's choice was Paul. This is untenable. Paul distinguishes himself from the twelve (see 1 Cor. 15:5,8). Scripture also states that on the Day of Pentecost, Peter stood up in the midst of eleven, God owning their choice of Matthias (see Acts 2:14). Also, Matthias was one of the twelve apostles who remained based in Jerusalem following the persecution that arose at the time of Stephen's death.

one of these, although he was unique amongst that first generation of post-ascension apostles in that he was part of the body of writers who gave us the New Testament revelation that clarifies our gospel—the inclusion of Gentiles in God's Church and restoration plan.

Scripture shows the Church having both doctrinal and *experiential* foundations. Its doctrinal foundation is Jesus and the twelve. But, *experientially*, every emerging church needs to *be in living fellowship with Christ and with a continuing apostolic and prophetic ministry*. Paul said that the apostles are part of the foundation in which Christ *Himself* is the chief cornerstone (see Eph. 2:20). They are not joined simply by what He said or taught, but with *Himself*, the person—a living relationship with the living Christ. Paul speaks of the apostolic ministry as laying a firm foundation of the revelation of Christ in the Church (see 1 Cor. 3:10-11).

Seeking to define the ministry of apostles in detail can be dangerous because it can lead us to cast them in inflexible molds and categories. Too frequently Paul becomes the sole measuring line for them, which goes beyond what can be biblically justified. Although it is true to say that Paul's apostolic commission is the one given the most detail in Scripture, the New Testament names several other post-ascension apostles as well.[2]

2. Notably, Barnabas, Andronicus and Junia, and Silas (see Acts 14:4,14; Rom. 16:7 KJV; 1 Thess. 1:1; 2:6).

The Restoration of Apostles and Prophets

There are various kinds of apostles. Although each apostle is sent with a specific commission, we are not told what his *gifting* is to accomplish it. Here lies a distinguishing mark between apostles. Some complete their task through prophetic gifting, others through teaching gifting, yet others from a mix of gifting. Apostles must remain sensitive to the Spirit and should not seek to "apostle" a situation in a field where the required gift is different to the one(s) recognized as their own. This is why, in this initial period of restoration of apostolic ministries and their relation to churches, there will be some measure of movement as the right apostles for the right groupings of people find each other. As such movement occurs, apostles must avoid foolish and immature feelings of rejection relating to the actions of elders and churches in response to other apostles. They must also avoid any feeling of superiority when people pursue relationship with them. We must recognize that people will respond to different gifts in different men. At the same time, we must remember what Paul wrote to the Corinthians in respect to apostolic involvement. Where there was a tendency for the people to divide between the apostles, Paul said, "*All* are yours" (1 Cor. 3:22). We, therefore, recognize that there are different kinds of apostles for different tasks and situations.

It is also important to realize that just like any other servants of God in ministry, apostles are also in the process of maturing in their gifting, wisdom, and authority. Apostles differ in these measures, which is why Paul spoke of apostles as having a "measure of rule" (see 2 Cor. 10:13 KJV), a "measure of faith" (Rom. 12:3), and a "measure" of God's gift (see Eph. 4:7 KJV). It is foolish for apostles to compare themselves with each other, or for people to compare apostle with apostle—just as it is foolish to compare teacher with teacher, pastor with pastor, evangelist with evangelist, or prophet with prophet. All ministries are in service to God and, through the processes of the Spirit, are in progress to maturity in their callings. It is time for the servants of God to stop being intimidated by people's preferences, prejudices, and childish games and to take seriously the responsibility of being faithful stewards and servants in the house of God.

While apostles are maturing in their calling, they may do the following:

1. *Fall short* (1 Cor. 10:12; Gal. 5:4)—Apostles may fail to complete the task to which they've been commissioned. This could happen for a variety of reasons, such as discouragement, immorality, love of money, jealousy, succumbing to wrong motivations, etc.

2. *Fall away* (2 Pet. 3:17)—It is even possible for apostles to abandon the faith through inner

conflict produced by mental or external pressure, demonic deception, and delusions of grandeur, or even through the despair and disappointment of hope deferred—much like Judas Iscariot.

3. *Become disqualified* (1 Cor. 9:27)—Paul became aware in his own ministry that his level of revelation and deep insight into the mysteries of God required him to set out his gospel to other ministries of depth and revelation so it could be tested and affirmed. He did not want to face the possibility, as he put it, of having "preached to others, I myself...be disqualified...."

4. *Fall victim to their own lack of watchfulness*—When Paul urged on the Ephesian elders in the light of his departure, knowing he would not see them again, he warned that they should "guard" themselves (see Acts 20:31). In so doing, he highlighted something imperative to all ministries. Paul knew the importance of sustaining his fellowship with God and of staying in the place where God could continually minister to and through him. He gave the Ephesian elders a principle that would enable this to happen for each of them: Guard yourself. Thousands of godly men have been willing to pour out their lives for the flock, only to fall victim themselves because they did not guard

themselves. Literally thousands of God's ministers have wearied in ministry, become jaded in life, experienced turmoil of mind, been devastated in their domestic situations, and seen their churches decline and be destroyed because of their failure to guard themselves. In giving this principle, Paul placed as much priority—if not even more—on keeping watch over oneself as much as the flock of God. This is why he said, "Keep watch over yourselves and all the flock of which the Holy Spirit has made you overseers" (Acts 20:28a).

What we are is more important than what we do, and guarding ourselves maintains our own inner spiritual abiding in Christ.

Apostles are called and appointed by Christ. They are not chosen by congregations, or even by fellow ministries (see Eph. 1:1; Col. 1:1; 2 Cor. 5:20). It also should be recognized that there might be a lengthy interval between what a person is *called* to be and what he or she is "*anointed*" or "*appointed*" to do. Paul was called to be an apostle on the Damascus road, and he received his commission to apostolic task in that initial encounter with Christ. He knew there and then that God was sending him to the Gentiles (nations) to open their eyes, to turn them from darkness to light and from the power of satan to God, and to enable them to receive their inheritance amongst the sanctified by faith in Christ (see Acts 26:18). All this was revealed to him in the life-changing encounter he had with God on the Damascus road; however, it was a further 17 years before he was separated to his commission (see Acts 9:1-7; 13:1-4).

It is a mistake to interpret a calling as a release to begin functioning. A deep awareness that one is called to be an apostle is not necessarily accompanied by other people's recognition of such. In other words, one cannot just go out and "apostle" situations. Jesus, the unique apostle, did not fully emerge in His ministry until He was 30 years old. He knew that He was called, but there came the time when He said, "The Spirit of the Lord is on Me, because He has anointed Me to…" (Lk. 4:18). He knew not only what He was, but also what He was anointed to do. There may be a large number of apostles who have received a genuine call from God, but they are not all appointed or anointed to do the same thing. We need to be patient and hold the confidence of our calling in Christ until the time comes when He anoints us clearly to our appointed task; then we can start functioning in our apostleship.

- *Apostles break new territory in the world* and establish the Church as an expression of the Kingdom in new cities and towns as they liberate men and women from their bonds and demonic control. They also bring order to the Body of Christ. The apostles and prophets, as the primary stewards of the mysteries of Christ, continuously measure the life and testimony of God's people against those mysteries. Where they find that the Church has deviated from God's purpose of restoration, they powerfully, prophetically, and demonstratively assert the purpose of God. They challenge any sectarian attitude or denominational spirit that threatens the unity of the Body. They bring judgment to any lifestyle contrary to the purity of Christ in the life of the believer. They confront powers of darkness that seek to introduce subtle legalisms and externalisms into the Body of Christ. And true apostles are willing and bold enough to confront each other—as Paul did Peter—whenever behavior is inconsistent with revelation (see Gal. 2:11-14).

- *Apostles rejoice and respond in every sovereign move of the Spirit that comes to refresh the Body*. They realize that each refreshing enables the people of God to find the strength and faith to continue their pilgrimage to fullness. Peter, for example, clearly shows the purpose of the "times of refreshing"; they are short seasons of divine renewal that lead the people of God toward the longer seasons of times of restoration (see Acts 3:19-21). In seasons of refreshing, apostles—by the wisdom of God—help the people of God see that the season of refreshing is a *transition*, and not the *terminus*. They keep the people *moving* in blessing and will not allow them to *settle* in that blessing.

- *Apostles have the necessary wisdom and authority of God to keep the Body of Christ both **filled** with truth and **walking** in it.* They, therefore, bring with their word a necessary element of judgment, so that the righteousness, peace, and joy of the Kingdom are maintained by an ever-present principle of judgment at work. Many times they may even bring a word to divide. People are afraid of the word *division*; they tend to think of it in exclusively negative terms. But frankly, division is a principle that God introduced in the very beginning. He *divided* the day from the night, the darkness from light, the waters above the earth from the waters below. The division of God in creation illustrates God's commitment to *clarity*. God does not allow His children to live in twilight. We are children of the day and not of the night. God abhors mixture.

- *Apostles and prophets will—by their ministry of Word and Spirit—keep the Church pure and progressing to fullness.* The product of their ministry will be that the glory of the House of God in this end-time will be seen as greater than in the history of Israel or the Church to date (see Hag. 2:9).

- *Apostles will strengthen and establish the Church of God when everything in our world is shaking.* They

127

explain the reason for what is happening and minister the principles and faith by which God's people will remain secure. God's shaking will go well beyond the Church—it will extend to all nations (see Dan. 2:44-45; Hag. 2:6-7). It will affect our world in every sphere: the economy, technological advances, scientific development, moral and social positions, and intellectual and educational establishments. Everything will shake until only the unshakable stands secure. The writer of Hebrews says, "We are receiving a kingdom that cannot be shaken" (Heb. 12:28). The apostles and prophets are at the forefront of leading God's people in the advance of the unshakable Kingdom of God in our generation.

All God's apostles are "*sent ones,*" not simply "men who go." Apostles are sent with a specific commission, and as such, they are empowered to act on behalf of the sender. At the same time we don't simply call someone an apostle because he *claims* to be sent. On the contrary, in the Book of Revelation churches are commended for *testing those who say they are apostles and are not* (see Rev. 2:2). In order for us to be secure in a relationship with apostles, we must know which ones are true as opposed to the ones who are false. Here are some common hallmarks that enable us to recognize true apostolic ministry.

Hallmarks of the Apostle and His Ministry

- A true apostle will have had a personal encounter with the resurrected Lord (see Acts 22:8).

- He will have been personally commissioned to an apostolic task (see Acts 26:16-18).

- He will fulfill his apostleship through some other gifting, for example, prophet, evangelist, or teacher (see Acts 13:1).

- He will be an equipper of the saints (see Eph. 4:11-12 NAS).

- He will be a good steward of the mysteries of God, of which he has a divine revelation (see Eph. 3:2-6).

- He will recognize and be recognized in his apostleship; that is, he may lead an apostolic team that emerges around him and proves to be a catalyst for other ministries. Conversely, he may be an apostle built into another apostle's sphere, as Barnabas was with Paul. A valid apostolic ministry does not necessarily have the same task as Paul's, in which one is the catalyst for many others.

- He will be a wise master builder (architect) of the House of God. An astute user of the plumb line of the mystery of Christ, he will measure everything that is built against the end purpose for the House (see 1 Cor. 3:10 NAS).

- He will demonstrate an apostle's authority given by Christ (see 2 Cor. 10:8).

- He will demonstrate grace and wisdom in his relationships with people so that a sphere of apostolic ministry and influence emerges in the lives of those people. His positive relations with the people of God will provide them with a deep sense of security. This will produce a committed, productive people who happily help him in the task he is called to. It is inside this sphere of committed people—those who are actively pursuing God's desire for His House—that the apostle has the authority of rule. This rule will not be exercised in some authoritarian manner or outside his sphere, but will follow the example of Christ, who came to serve rather than be served (see Mt. 20:25-28).

- He is a man pursuing a vision in which he is:
    i. *Clear* as to what he has seen in his *commission*;
    ii. *Committed* to its completion;
    iii. *Obedient* to the will of God in its commands; and
    iv. *Patiently persevering* in obedience to the heavenly vision despite any and all setbacks.

An apostolic commission is fulfilled in phases; it is a process. With the completion of each phase the apostle will be sensitive to God's "sending" into the new phase (see Acts 14:26). When all phases of his apostolic commission are complete he will be able to say, as did the apostle Paul, "I have finished the race" (2 Tim. 4:7). He can then with joy be received by the Lord for his reward.

- He is filled with persevering faith. Regardless of enticements, setbacks, or opposition from men or demons, the apostle's faith enables him to persevere. This faith will extend itself to lay hold of all that is necessary from the supply of God's grace to fulfill his ministry and to lay hold of the people and money resource required for the task. His faith will demonstrate the supernatural power of God so that God is seen to be working with him confirming His Word with signs and wonders following (see Mk. 16:20).

- The apostle will be the living example of all that he wants the people to become and do. Therefore, his personal Christlikeness will be evident to all so that they are secure in following his example. He may unashamedly stand before the people and say, "You yourselves know how you ought to follow us" (see 2 Thess. 3:7-9). He is humble and a man of prayer. His longsuffering gentleness with the weak, his firmness with those who require it, and his integrity and honesty in business matters and dealings with people should all speak well of him.

- He is focused in Christ and does not boast of his own status (see Rom. 3:27; 1 Thess. 2:6).

- Paul refers to the apostles as being set forward "first of all" and "last of all" (see 1 Cor. 4:9 KJV; 1 Cor. 12:28). Apostles are the *first* among the ministries in building the Church of God, because they lay a foundation of understanding concerning the mystery of Christ. Yet, in terms of people's affection and recognition, they are frequently *last* of all and are often treated as "the refuse" of society (in Peterson's terms, "potato peelings from the culture's kitchen"[3]). In human terms, they are the *first in responsibility* and the *last in reward*.

Prophets

It is unfortunate that people's concept of a prophet is so frequently colored by their view of John the Baptist, with his camel hair clothing and diet of locusts and wild honey. The image many people have of a prophet is an austere, aesthetic individual who is oddly dressed and tends to live in strange places. Happily, the Bible introduces a much wider range of prophets than John the Baptist, beginning with Abel (see Lk. 11:50-51), continuing through the biblical record with such people as Abraham, Moses, Samuel, and David, and right on through into the New Covenant with Anna, Agabus, Silas, Judas, etc. Rather

---

3. Eugene Peterson, *The Message* (Colorado Springs, Colorado: NavPress, 1995), 1 Cor. 4:9.

than building a mental image out of varied physical details of different prophets, it is much more productive to look at other factors in understanding a prophet's ministry.

Prophets can be described in the following ways:

- *People of God's presence.* They know what it is to enter the spiritual world of God's throne room presence *to hear the voice of God's counsel and to see a situation from God's perspective.* They understand what it is to stand silent and attentive in the council of God, which is why God always shows His ways to the prophets and encourages His people to heed them (see Jer. 23:18,22; Is. 29:10; Amos 3:7; 2 Pet. 1:19-21; Rev. 1:3,9-10; 4:1-2).

- *People of perception.* Neither the eyes nor the mind of a prophet are imprisoned by the visible world. The prophets were originally called *seers* (see 1 Sam. 9:9), and they not only see situations, but also hearts. They are able to apply the Word of God to the visible situation by the understanding and perception that they gain of it in the invisible world. The visible and invisible worlds appear as one to them. A classic example of this is Elisha's peace as he lay on the bed after his servant had warned him the Assyrians had surrounded him in the night (see 2 Kings 6:15). He simply prayed that God would open the servant's eyes and release him from his imprisonment to the material and tangible world in which we live. When the servant went out and looked, he was astonished to see the hosts of God surrounding the Assyrian army. His excited report was met with the prophet's calm response: "Those who are with us are more than those who are with them" (2 Kings 6:16).

- *People of revelation.* Paul highlighted this understanding and depiction of the value of prophetic ministry in the Church. Along with apostles, prophets have understanding and wisdom in the mystery of Christ (see Eph. 3:4-5; 1 Cor. 14:28-30). They join with apostles in laying the foundation of understanding and practiced truth; they both establish it and *are* it.

- *People of confrontation.* Prophets—emboldened with the word of God and anointed by God's Spirit—are not afraid to confront authorities and/or situations. Nathan disturbed David's comfort zone by exposing David's sin in taking Bathsheba and having her husband Uriah killed at the military front line (see 2 Sam. 11–12). Moses, who spent 40 years being reduced in his own mind from an articulate, skilled prince of Egypt to a mere desert shepherd, nevertheless stood before Pharaoh and, emboldened with God's word, cried out, "Let My people go" (Ex. 5:1). John the Baptist confronted Herod with the sinfulness of taking Herod's brother's wife, ultimately paying for his stand with his life (see Mk. 6:17-28). *Prophets deliver the word of God* in spite of the possible or predictable consequences.

- *People of demonstration. Authentic prophets are the embodiment of the word that they are carrying.* Before they call for people to come into alignment with God's will and purpose, they are themselves living in that will and purpose. Their lives are characterized by commitment to God's heart and rule in all things. They are passionate for righteousness and justice. Their primary concerns are God's interests. This is why God is secure in His prophets to the point that He implied that He wouldn't do anything without first telling them (see Amos 3:7).

- *People of motivation.* Passionately enthused by the word and Spirit of God, prophets are able to inspire the faith of God's people and motivate them to pursue the task God sets before them. This is demonstrated in the time of Haggai during the rebuilding of the temple, when those living in nostalgia for the first temple discouraged the people from rebuilding. Haggai came and passionately cried, " 'I am with you,' declares the Lord" (Hag. 1:13-14). This was hardly a dynamic new revelation! But it was *a powerful inspiration and motivation when spoken in the passion of an anointed prophet.*

- *People of perseverance.* Not only do prophets motivate, but they are also committed to seeing the word of God accomplish its purpose. They continue to provoke the people with God's current word, keeping their hope alive and their faith active until the will of God is accomplished (see Amos 9:11-15; Acts 15:12-18; see also the entire books of Ezra, Zechariah, and Haggai).

Prophets are passionate for the interests of God. There is nothing mediocre about these men and women. Everything about their life is passionate—what they hate they hate absolutely; what they love they love absolutely. What they do knows no half-measure. There is an edge to their sword, a conviction in their tone of voice. This is what we need today; we need prophetic fervor, not simply a prophetic flavor.

It is our ability to passionately identify with God's purpose that qualifies us, as Paul said, to "all prophesy" (see 1 Cor. 14:31).

It is the failure to sustain a prophetic passion for God's purpose of restoration that has given us a "Christianity of the trivial," which pays more attention to performance than proclamation. We have elders who are trapped in the busyness of barrenness, occupied with peripheral activities and administration rather than with preparing their hearts to prophesy to the people or to be sensitive to their hurts and cry.

The Restoration of Apostles and Prophets

The failure to sustain prophetic passion has allowed Christianity to dissolve into a competitive scramble by the small-minded to relate a few more to their cause, as opposed to working in harmony to advance the Kingdom, disciple the people, and pursue God's purpose of unity in the bonds of peace.

As we cross the line into a third millennium, if we are to see an effective, dynamic testimony of authentic Christianity in every city and town in our nation, then we must prevail in prayer for God to give us a fresh wave of passionate prophets.

God has not gifted men and women to do everything for a largely sedentary Church. The purpose of prophets, as well as those in other ministry callings, is to *equip the saints for the work of the ministry* (see Eph. 4:12 NRS). This is one of the primary functions of apostles and prophets. Engaged in a program larger than expressing their own giftedness, *they enable others to move in the gifts*. In this fundamental way, they contribute to God's purpose in regeneration, restoration, and reformation.

As God is restoring apostles and prophets in the Church, I have heard it said in various countries, "I believe God will raise up *our own* apostles and prophets. We don't need to be dependent on British apostles or American prophets." This thinking has no place in the one holy nation of God. The Bible does not say that God has set in the Church British apostles, South African prophets, American evangelists, and German teachers; rather, it says that God has set *in the Church* apostles, prophets, evangelists, pastors, and teachers. They are distinguished by their giftings and anointing in Christ. Any failure to change these attitudes will hold up our progress toward maturity and seeing the power of God break through in the churches.

Ministers of Christ in Our World

Our world is a highly complex one made up of many spheres (worlds) of interest—world politics, economics, business, law, medicine, education, sports, and theater, to name just a few. Generally, to be a voice of influence in any one of these spheres requires proper positioning within its framework. For example, a highly trained and experienced member of the legal profession is better positioned and would be given a better hearing on matters of law and justice than someone trained in agriculture. Similarly, those engaged in research in medical fields associated with problems in the food chain will find their opinions carry more weight in a food poisoning scare than someone who is a quiz show host. In other words, *to maximize one's influence in any field, one needs to specialize in it.* God understands this perfectly. In sending us into the world He wants us to penetrate each of its spheres (worlds). *We need to "go deeper" into our chosen sphere of interest as servants of God, not come out of them in order to become a servant.*

When God commissioned the Church to "go into all the world" (Mk. 16:15), He meant for us to penetrate each sphere of it with a living expression of His mind and will. Restorers believe that God's intention is to have apostles, prophets, evangelists, pastors, and teachers who are politicians, business persons, sports personalities, actors, computer engineers, and so on rather than becoming a professional religious clergy trapped in a professional religious ghetto. We must recover our understanding of these ministry callings in the context of God's purpose to fill the earth with His image and likeness. Only in this way will Christians truly salt and light our world at every level of human contact and communication.

To tell young men and women that they *must* give up their jobs to "serve the Lord" has delayed the evangelization of our world and robbed its institutional structures of the impact of the Kingdom of God. There are some people whom God wants given entirely to a specific ministry that is so demanding they would be unable to fulfill it and hold down a job at the same time. When such people then give up their job to pursue their calling it is both understandable and seen as necessary, but it is not the norm. The heart cry of the restorer is, "Lord, You have sent Your Church into our world to bring Your Kingdom to men and women, and You have given Your Church apostles, prophets, evangelists, pastors, and teachers. Lord, raise them up as artists, inventors, scientists, medics, teachers, professors, lawyers, judges, business men and women, journalists, industrialists, actors, storekeepers, athletes, and provide every other role of service in our world."

Imagine what a difference it will make when many scriptwriters, producers, and directors of major theater and film productions are Christians with a concern for the well-being of the family as their pastoral calling or with a desire to introduce unbelievers to faith in Christ as an evangelist. What changes there will be when multi-national corporations, stock exchanges, and commodity boards have committed Christian leaders in the top echelons of their executive leadership, leaders who have the strategic mind of the apostle, the foreseeing eye of the prophet, and the compassion of God's heart. The business world will be an entirely different place. How dramatic the effect will be on the general populace when such men and women fulfill their callings in and through the Church in the world.

In response to the crises we face in our educational systems, welfare organizations, prisons, and inner cities, people are not crying out for more government intrusion, more state-initiated programs, or more money to be thrown at the problems. Instead, they are seeking wisdom, commitment, and moral leadership in every field. Cosmetic changes, empty promises, regurgitated political policies, and additional "inquiries"—all announced with articulate fanfare—only lead to more disillusionment, frustration, and reaction in the general populace.

We need to awake to the hour. We are not God's people in a vacuum, but God's people sent to a world in crisis. The harvest is not inside four walls vibrating with hymns or choruses, but in our streets, hospitals, prisons, clubs, and workplaces. Christians need to embrace the implications of the call of *God that has sent us into the world* (see Jn. 17:18). Apostolic wisdom, prophetic insight and passion, evangelistic zeal, pastoral concern and care, and the teacher's ability to instruct and train, are all required to play their part in seeing men and women transformed and society reformed.

It is with this in mind that we gain a deeper appreciation of Paul's use of the term *body*. When Jesus came into the world, He cried, *"A body You have prepared for Me...I have come to do Your will, O God"* (Heb. 10:5-7 NRS). God, who is invisible Spirit, entered a body of flesh. Now that Christ has returned to the Father in Heaven, God has prolonged His days in a new Body, the Church, a corporate people (see Is. 53:10).

It is through this corporate Body that God expresses His heart and will for mankind.

Our gifting not only benefits, blesses, and matures the Church, but is also the means through which God ministers His life to all. In practice, this means that the greater manifestation of the gifts of the Spirit in our experience will be in the day-to-day course of our lives. Jesus makes Himself known in and through us in the everyday marketplace of life on the streets of the twenty-first century. His life is not confined to religious meetings, for He moves, blesses, and heals through us as we daily go to where the masses of people are to be found.

How Can We Be More Effective in This Arena?

1. *Every day give your mind, your emotions, and your body over to God as a vehicle through which He can express Himself.* Pray that your heart will feel what His heart is feeling, that your mind will be filled with what His mind is intending, and that your eyes, ears, lips, and hands will be available to Him through which He may see, hear, speak to, and bless those whose lives you touch.

2. *Step out into your day expecting God to respond to your yielded life.* Christians should get on the bus, train, or car, or walk into the office, store, factory, university, or children's school fully expecting God to bless them and make them a blessing that day.

3. *Live confidently and boldly, responding with a childlike faith to the promptings of His Spirit.* Understand that whatever God is telling you to do, He will be with you in the doing of it. Whatever the consequences of any bold action you take, you can be sure that God was not only with you in prompting the action, but also remains with you in the consequences of the action you have taken.

4. *Never seek to take the applause to yourself.* People's gratitude undoubtedly follows miracles, help, and success. Always give God the direct praise and glory for what has taken place. In this way you make certain of a continued experience of union and life with God in the supernatural.

When Jesus stepped out each day it was with a conscious sense of the presence of God with Him. He had taken specific time to seek the Father's mind and will in the "secret place" (see Mt. 6:4-6). It was in the secret place that Jesus would often see the Father doing things or that His spirit would hear the Father say things, and instantly He would know that what He was seeing and hearing of the Father was what the Father wanted Him to do (see Jn. 5:19). As a consequence, He walked the streets of the villages and cities fully anticipating that He would be used to bring God's life to people by the Spirit. *His heart was prepared by the Spirit in the secret place for what the Spirit wished to do through Him in the public place.*

We are not above Jesus; if He needed time alone with God in the secret place, how much more do we? (See Matthew 10:24-25.) Jesus directly accused the Pharisees of trying to steal praise for themselves and showed them that they would never move in the supernatural because they would not be able to receive the faith required for it. Their self-interest and desire for praise and glory from each other prevented unity with the Father (see Jn. 5:44).

This third millennium will undoubtedly see an acceleration of research and learning, which in turn means new technologies, scientific advances, and global changes affecting the lifestyle of our peoples. The Church of God is not meant to be running behind, desperately trying to catch up with the world. Rather it is to be at the forefront of the quest for moral direction, providing biblical interpretation for the advances produced.

The Word of God is timeless in the sense that it stands in God outside of time, yet speaks to every moment of time. It was valid to 2.5 million Israelites on the day they moved out of Egypt, and it is equally valid today for 5.5 billion who globally are seeking to find "straight paths" in a disordered society. It was not only a lamp for the feet and a light to the path for the Psalmist (see Ps. 119:105), but is equally so for us in these darkening days (see Phil. 2:15) of the third millennium in human history.

Conclusion

What I have attempted to do in this book is to disturb our comfort zones, challenge our thoughts, and give us a vision of a community of God that lives on a higher level than that of Christian trivia. God is looking for a people aware that they are born for such a time as this, aware that it is upon this generation that the end of time has come. As this people, we know that inside the grace of God He has chosen us in particular to be His voice and testimony in the closing of an age (see 1 Cor. 10:11; 1 Pet. 4:7).

We are deeply conscious not only of the moment in which we live, but also of the call of the Spirit to respond with a sharp vision, a quickened faith, and a willing heart to the challenge of this hour.

Whatever religious baggage we have carried until now, if it is not relevant to life or to ministering life, is to be discarded. This radical hour in human history calls for radical men and women to stand and speak up for Christ. In this sense, His "sons and daughters will prophesy" (Acts 2:17). It is not the time to weigh the "pros and cons" of obedience or to examine the possible outcomes and consequences of a radical stance. Our generation—blinded by pleasurable wickedness, committed only to its own self-preservation and good, hedonistic in its approach to living, rejecting Christ and ignoring God *en masse*—will never be impacted in its conscience or moved to consider covenantal change unless we, the Church of God, show in our lives and declare in our words the necessity and blessing of belonging to Christ.

Tomorrow's world belongs to those who today have been caught up into its larger purpose and program. It belongs to those who understand that they are born into something already going on, something in which they have a significant part to play. This is not a parochial view of those trapped in limited vision. They work inside the context of a cosmic view of life, constantly seeing the immediate in the light of the ultimate. By their faith they keep pushing out the boundaries of life, not allowing themselves to be trapped by the success of their previous achievements. They have learned to distinguish between the temporal and the eternal, never allowing the latter to be jeopardized by the former. They have been careful in their choice of relationship to be sure it is with those who share the common vision and destiny. They don't run with those who will trap them in the smallness of the world of fading dreams and mean hopes. But rather they run with those who challenge them to greater things, whose faith and zeal are as iron sharpening iron (see Prov. 27:17). In pressing on, they know what to forget and what to remember, what to leave behind and what to carry forward.

I am convinced, in reading the Scriptures, that preceding the return of Jesus Christ, such a generation of committed Christians will emerge. It is these people who will provide "the line of faith" for Christ's reentry into this time-space world. It is this generation's response in obedience of faith to the radical nature of the gospel that will cause the world to re-examine itself and seek after God. It is this generation that will hasten the day of His coming (see 2 Pet. 3:12). Let's not project what I am saying to the future; ours is the opportunity and privilege of rising in faith to this call now. We can be that people that collectively rejects the compromised, neutralized lifestyle of mediocre Christianity and instead becomes a people of burning hearts passionately advancing the Kingdom of God across the earth.

Other
Destiny Image titles
you will enjoy reading

ENCOUNTERING THE PRESENCE
by Colin Urquhart.
What is it about Jesus that, when we encounter Him, we are changed? When we encounter the Presence, we encounter the Truth, because Jesus is the Truth. Here Colin Urquhart, best-selling author and pastor in Sussex, England, explains how the Truth changes facts. Do you desire to become more like Jesus? The Truth will set you free!
ISBN 0-7684-2018-0

THE GOD CHASERS (Best-selling **Destiny Image** book)
by Tommy Tenney.
Are you dissatisfied with "church"? Are you looking for more? Do you yearn to touch God? You may be a *God chaser*! The passion of Tommy Tenney, evangelist and third-generation Pentecostal minister, is to "catch" God and find himself in God's manifest presence. For too long God's children have been content with crumbs. The Father is looking for those who will seek His face. This book will enflame your own desire to seek God with your whole heart and being—and to find Him.
ISBN 0-7684-2016-4

THE POWER OF BROKENNESS
by Don Nori.
Accepting Brokenness is a must for becoming a true vessel of the Lord, and is a stepping-stone to revival in our hearts, our homes, and our churches. Brokenness alone brings us to the wonderful revelation of how deep and great our Lord's mercy really is. Join this companion who leads us through the darkest of nights. Discover the *Power of Brokenness*.
ISBN 1-56043-178-4

AUDIENCE OF ONE
by Jeremy and Connie Sinnott.
More than just a book about worship, *Audience of One* will lead you into experiencing intimacy and love for the only One who matters—your heavenly Father. Worship leaders and associate pastors themselves, Jeremy and Connie Sinnott have been on a journey of discovering true spiritual worship for years. Then they found a whole new dimension to worship—its passion, intimacy, and love for the Father, your *audience of One*.
ISBN 0-7684-2014-8

Available at your local Christian bookstore.

nternet: http://www.reapernet.com